A–Z OF THE COTSWOLDS
Places - People - History

Sue Hazeldine

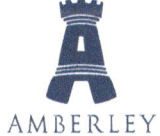

First published 2022

Amberley Publishing
The Hill, Stroud, Gloucestershire, GL5 4EP
www.amberley-books.com

Copyright © Sue Hazeldine, 2022

The right of Sue Hazeldine to be identified as the Author of this work has been asserted in accordance with the Copyrights, Designs and Patents Act 1988.

ISBN 978 1 4456 9374 3 (print)
ISBN 978 1 4456 9375 0 (ebook)

All rights reserved. No part of this book may be reprinted or reproduced or utilised in any form or by any electronic, mechanical or other means, now known or hereafter invented, including photocopying and recording, or in any information storage or retrieval system, without the permission in writing from the Publishers.

British Library Cataloguing in Publication Data.
A catalogue record for this book is available from the British Library.

Typesetting by SJmagic DESIGN SERVICES, India. Printed in Great Britain.

Contents

Adlestrop	5	Jurassic Way	42
Amberley	6		
		Kelmscott	43
Berkeley	8	Kingscote	44
Bibury	10		
Bisley	11	Lechlade	45
Burford	12	Lower Slaughter	46
Castle Combe	14	Malmesbury	47
Cheltenham	15	Minster Lovell	48
Chipping Campden	17		
Cirencester	18	Nailsworth	51
		Northleach	52
Daglingworth	20		
Deddington	21	Oddington	54
Dover's Hill	22	Owlpen	55
Down Ampney	24	Ozleworth	56
The Duntisbournes	25		
		Painswick	58
Eastleach Martin and Eastleach Turville	27	Prinknash Abbey	61
Ebrington	28		
Elkstone	29	Quenington	62
		Quinton, Upper and Lower	63
Fairford	30		
Filkins	31	Randwick	65
		Rodborough	66
Gloucester	32	Rodmarton	67
Guiting Power	34	Rollright Stones	68
Hailes Abbey	35	Sapperton	69
Hetty Pegler's Tump	36	Sezincote	70
Hidcote	37	Slimbridge	71
Horton Court	38	Stow-on-the-Wold	73
		Stroud	75
Icomb	40	Sudeley	76
Ilmington	41		

A-Z of the Cotswolds

Tetbury	78	Witney	89
Tewkesbury	79		
Tyndale Monument	80	X – Crossroads: Tom Long's Signpost	92
Uley	82	Yanworth	94
Vales	84	Zebras in the Cotswolds	95
Villas	84		
		Acknowledgements	96
Whittington	87		
Winchcombe	88		

Adlestrop

Yes, I remember Adlestrop –
The name, because one afternoon
Of heat the express train drew up there
Unwontedly, it was late June.

The steam hissed. Someone cleared his throat.
No one left and no one came
On the bare platform. What I saw
Was Adlestrop – only the name

And willows, willow-herb, and grass
And meadowsweet, and haycocks dry,
No whit less still and lonely fair
Than the high cloudlets in the sky.

And for that minute a blackbird sang
Close by, and round him, mistier
Farther and farther, all the birds
Of Oxfordshire and Gloucestershire.

Edward Thomas

'Adlestrop' is one of Edward Thomas's best-known poems; in fact it has made the village a household name. It describes a break in his journey between Hereford and Paddington on 24 June 1914. Of course Adlestrop station was a casualty of Dr Beeching's cuts to rural railways in 1966, but the large station sign and Thomas's evocative poem have a place in a bus shelter on the edge of the village, commemorating a more tranquil period in Adlestrop's past. Thomas was killed at Arras and his poem was published just three weeks later. Another literary connection is the Revd Thomas Leigh who was the cousin of Jane Austen's mother and rector of Adlestrop for fifty-one

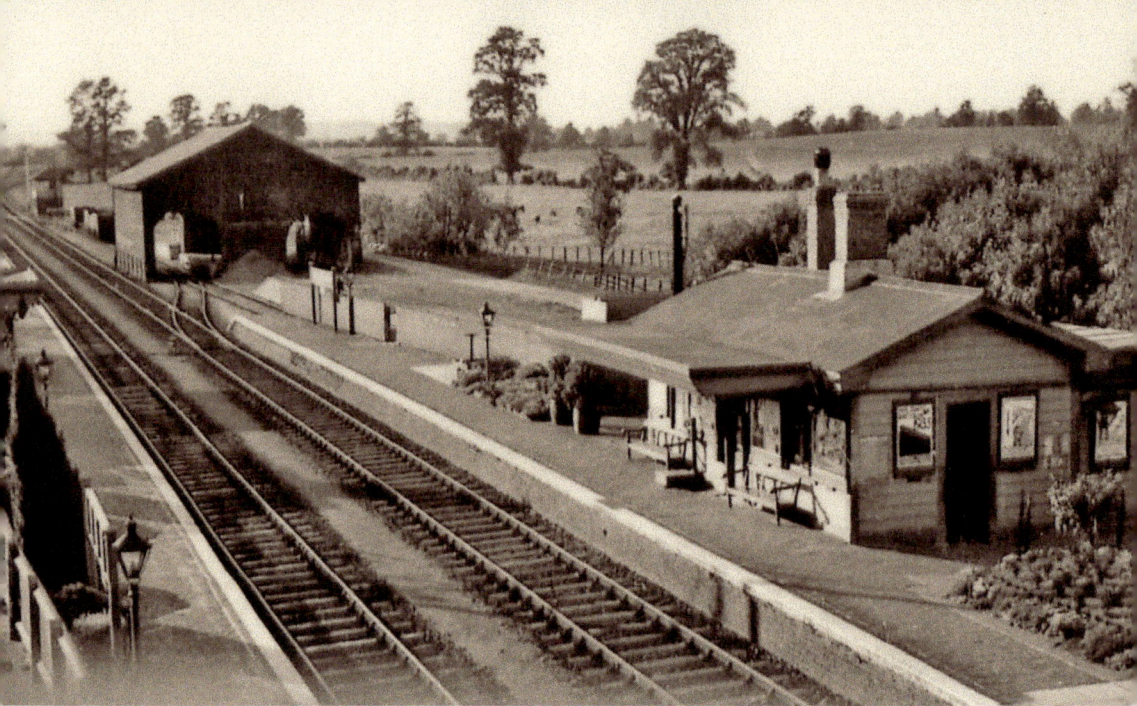

Adlestrop station.

years. Austen visited Adlestrop House, the fine rectory opposite the church, several times between 1794 and 1806 while Humphrey Repton was at work on the rectory garden. She expresses her disapproval of garden improvement in *Mansfield Park*!

Amberley

In the corner of Minchinhampton Common, 1 mile north of Nailsworth, lies the village of Amberley. In the nineteenth century it was here that Mrs Dinah Maria Craik (née Mulock) wrote her novel *John Halifax, Gentleman* while convalescing at Rose Cottage.

'We wound down the slope, and came in front of Rose Cottage. It was well named. I never in my life had seen such a bush of bloom. They hung in clusters – those roses – a dozen in a group, pressing their pinky cheeks together in a mass of family fragrance, pushing in at the parlour window, climbing up to the very attic.'

John Halifax, Gentleman is truly a novel of its time, given over to Victorian sentimentality about death. It has references to Shakespeare and Byron, as well as Dr Jenner and vaccination when smallpox infiltrates the family home. Even the date of the abolition of slavery is touched upon. John is an innovator who introduces steam power into the workings of his cloth mill when Lord Luxmore hijacks the mill stream to feed his own fountains – but he always has the welfare of his workers at heart, thus avoiding the uprising of workers displaced by the introduction of new technology. Amusingly, elsewhere the dangers of the newfangled steam railway are mentioned. John inherited the cloth mills through marriage to Ursula, an heiress of higher rank, but he always acknowledged that he was as good as any man in the land. *John Halifax,*

Gentleman is a Victorian morality tale, as the hero rises through the ranks through his own hard work and fierce integrity: 'Everybody knew him, everybody smiled as he passed, as though his presence and recognition were good things to have and to win.'

A plaque to Mrs Craik was placed in Tewkesbury Abbey – although not a native to Gloucestershire – by her fellow writers Lord Tennyson, Robert Browning and Matthew Arnold, amongst others, out of respect for her as a writer. *John Halifax, Gentleman* remained her most popular work.

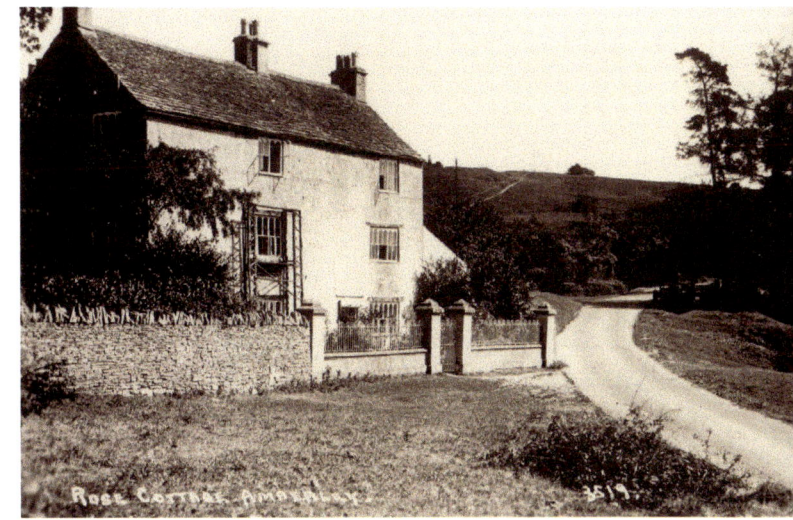

Right: Rose Cottage, Amberley.

Below: Rose Cottage.

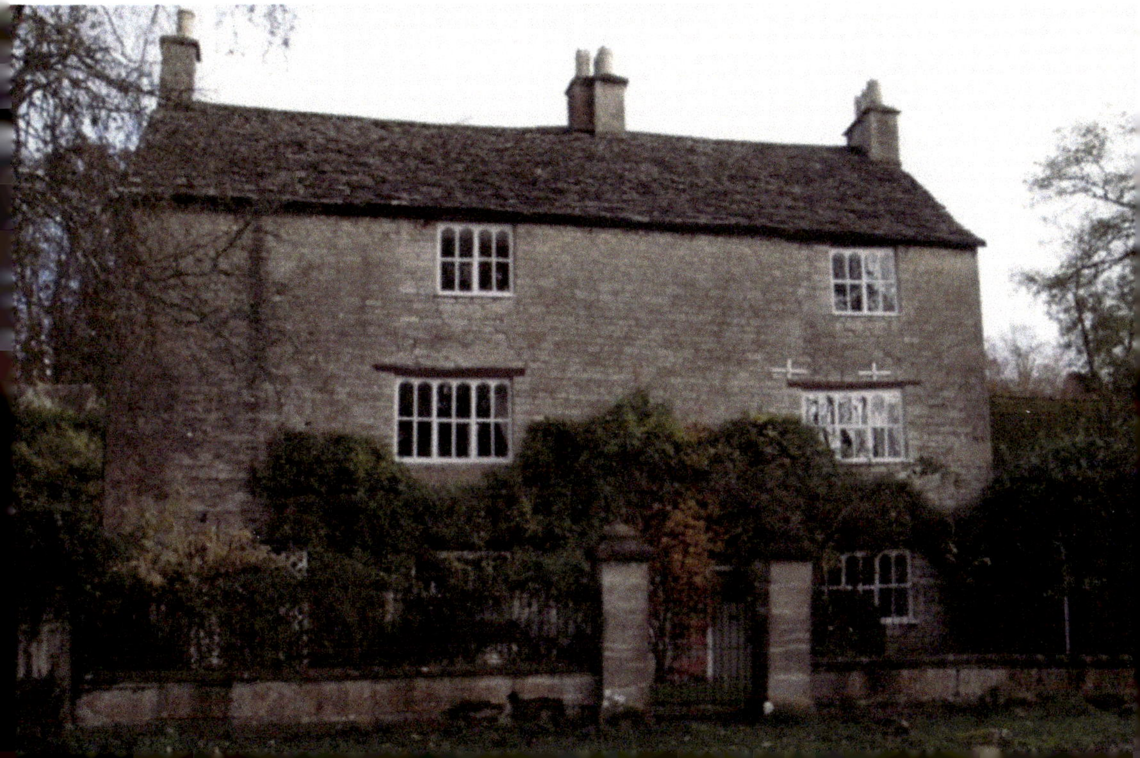

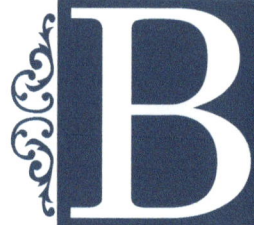

Berkeley

In the Middle Ages Berkeley (a clearing in the birchwood) was a port and market town. In 1067 the Earl of Hereford, William Fitzosbern, built a castle here. It is mostly twelfth century. In 1153 it was granted to Robert Fitzharding by Henry II. The Berkeleys are descended from Fitzharding and it remains in their hands to this very day.

More additions were made to the building in the fourteenth century. The Berkeley Hunt was founded in 1067, and is the oldest hunt in England. The huntsmen wear distinctive yellow coats rather than the usual 'pink' or black. It is said that Berkeley lands spread from Gloucestershire to Berkeley Square in London. In the eighteenth century Elizabeth Drax, a Berkeley wife, took exception to the appearance of the kennels and a façade had to be built to disguise the building.

Within the rosy-walled keep is the Great Hall, the morning room, and the dungeon where Edward II was brutally killed in 1327 – a red-hot poker was inserted into his rectum so that no visible signs of injury would be present. It was also suggested that the punishment fitted the crime as Edward had been having an affair with Piers Gaveston. Edward II's tomb can be found in Gloucester Cathedral, previously the abbey church, where it became something of a shrine.

It is thought that Shakespeare penned *A Midsummer Night's Dream* for the wedding of Sir Thomas Berkeley to Elizabeth Carey in February 1596. Berkeley is also mentioned in *Richard II* when Bolingbroke asks, 'How far is it, my Lord, to Berkeley now?' It is quite possible that the playwright was familiar with the region.

During the Civil War the castle was captured by the Parliamentarian Colonel Thomas Rainsborough in 1645. There was a siege when cannon were fired from the church roof. The walls were breached but the Berkeleys were able to retain ownership provided they did not repair the keep and bailey by Act of Parliament. Damage can still be seen on the church tower which stands apart from the main body of the church.

Berkeley Castle is the third oldest castle that has been continuously occupied by the same family after the Tower of London and Windsor Castle. Not only that but there is also an antique four-poster bed at the castle which has been in continuous use by the same family for the longest time in the UK.

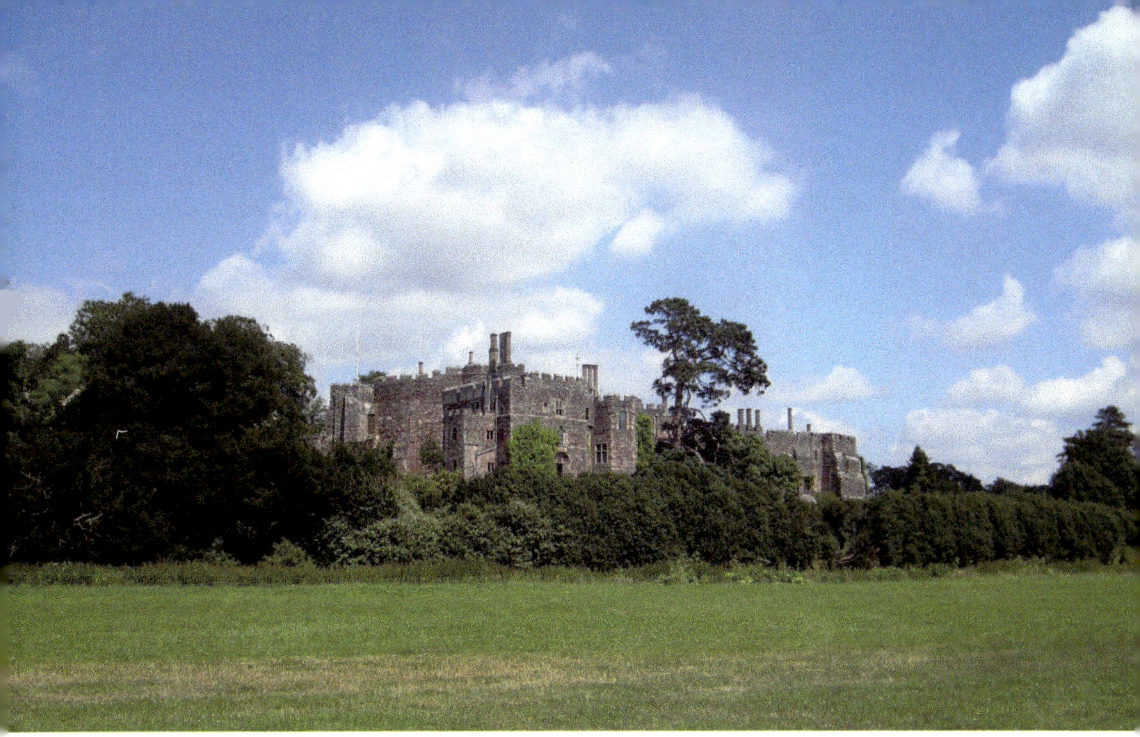

Above: Berkeley Castle.

Below: Berkeley Castle kennels.

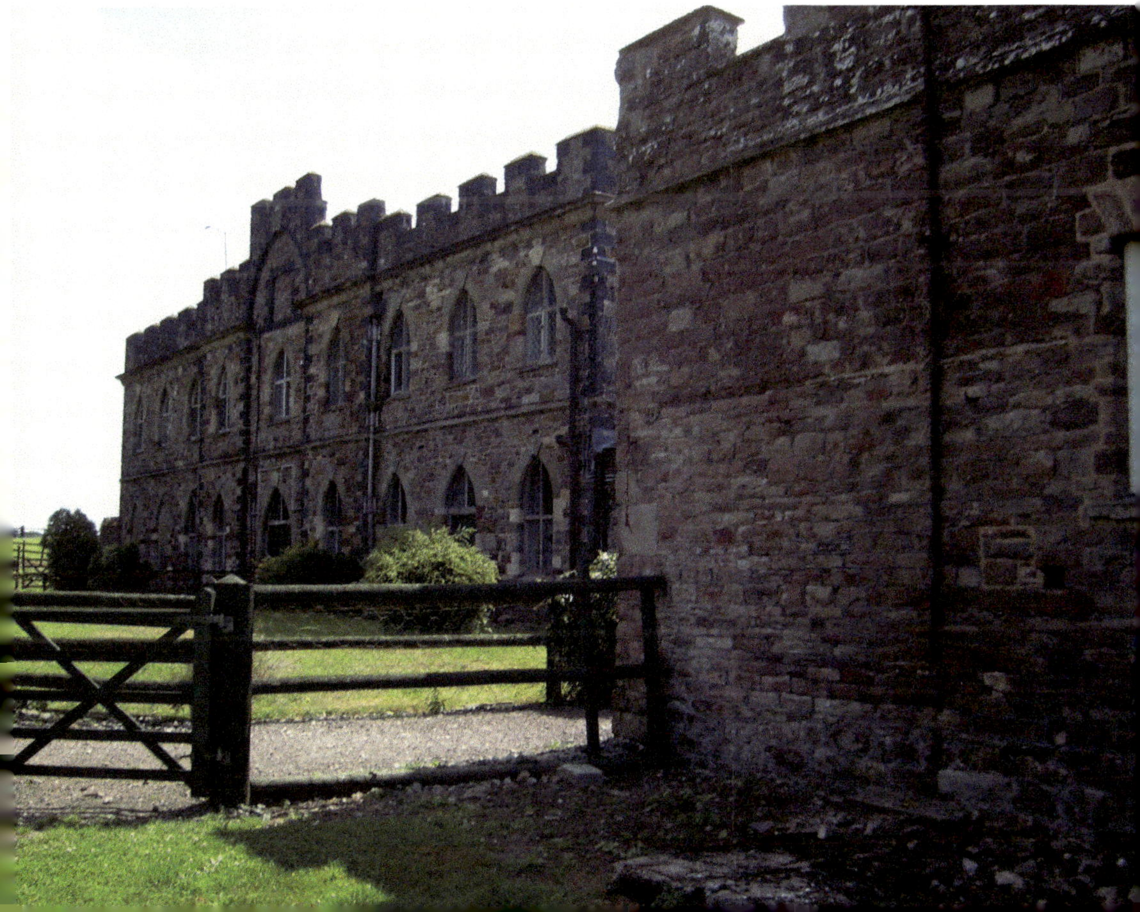

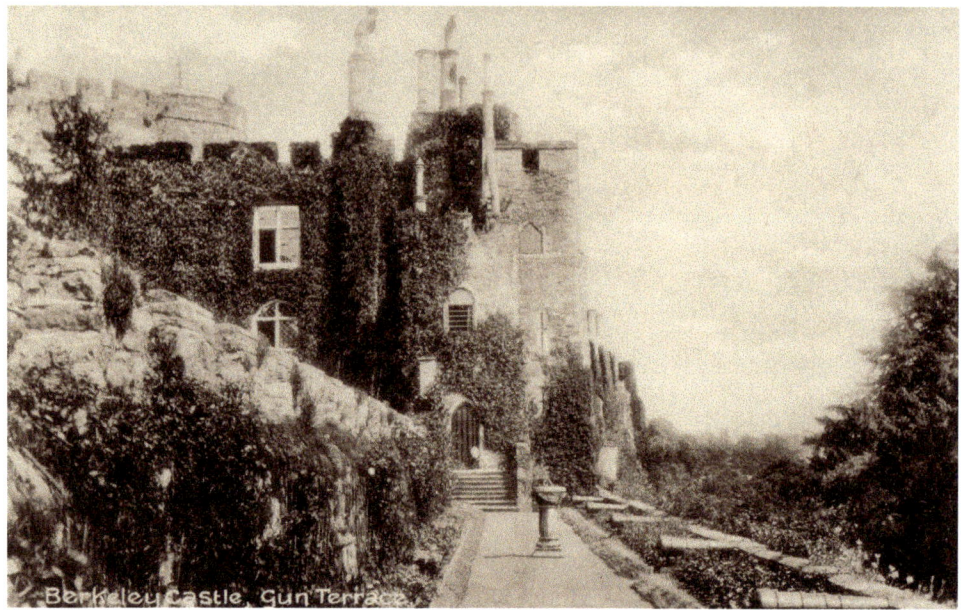

Berkeley Castle.

Bibury

Built in 1380, Bibury's Arlington Row was a sheep shelter for Osney Abbey in Oxford. It became a medieval wool store but in the seventeenth century was converted to weavers' cottages for workers of Arlington Mill – the dormer windows threw light on the weavers' work. In one cottage there is a tank for washing and dyeing cloth.

The quaint and picturesque Arlington Row accounts for Bibury's place on many a calendar and no doubt contributed to William Morris's opinion that Bibury was 'the most beautiful village in England'. It certainly caught Henry Ford's fancy when he saw it. He had plans to dismantle it and transport it to America where it would be rebuilt as part of a museum in Detroit similar to the Science Museum in London, which he greatly admired. Fortunately for us the Society of Arts intervened and prevented this plan from going ahead, so Ford had to content himself with the substitutes of Rose Cottage in Chedworth and a blacksmith's shop at Snowshill.

Rack Isle, the wild area in front of Arlington Row, is where there would once have been frames where firstly wool and then woven cloth was put out to dry and finally stretched to the correct dimensions. Here grew all sorts of damp-loving plants, as they do now – the water of the Coln flows around the edge of the field, arising from a spring in the grounds of the Swan Hotel. The water is crystal clear and supports trout and all sorts of waterfowl, and enhances the beauty of the village.

Arlington Row is now in the hands of the National Trust and it is even possible to stay in one of the cottages as a holiday destination.

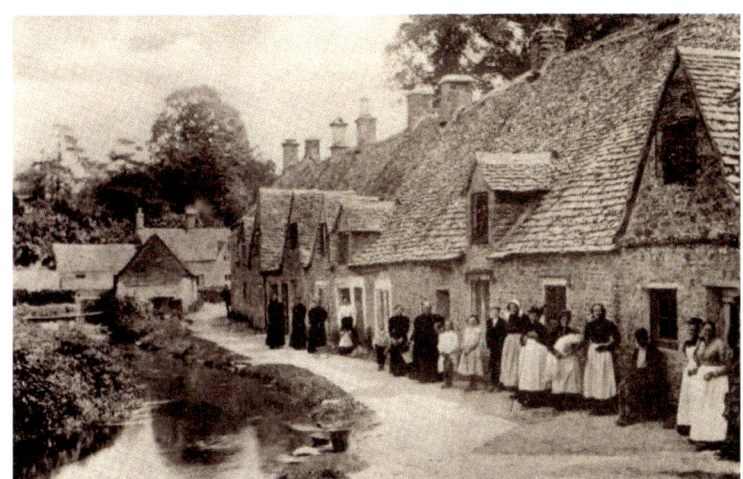

Arlington Row, Bibury.

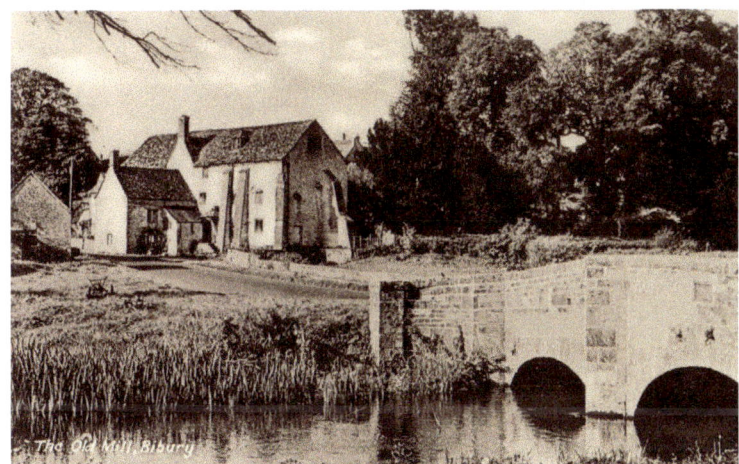

The Mill, Bibury.

Bisley

Of the many beautiful villages in the area Bisley must be one of the most desirable with its collection of seventeenth- and eighteenth-century stone cottages with Cotswold-tiled roofs. It is here that the racy novelist Jilly Cooper chose to make her home, and Mike Oldfield his studio. It boasts a village lock-up, a set of well heads below the church, an ancient poor light in the churchyard and an intriguing legend: it is said that as a ten-year-old girl Elizabeth I lived at Over Court where unfortunately she sickened and died. To conceal this sad event from the irascible Henry VIII a local boy was substituted to take her place – hence her reputation as the 'Virgin Queen'. It seems that a young girl's skeleton was actually unearthed in a stone coffin near Over Court and the overheated imaginations of Canon Keble's son Thomas and his friends supplied the rest, which became 'the legend of the Bisley boy'.

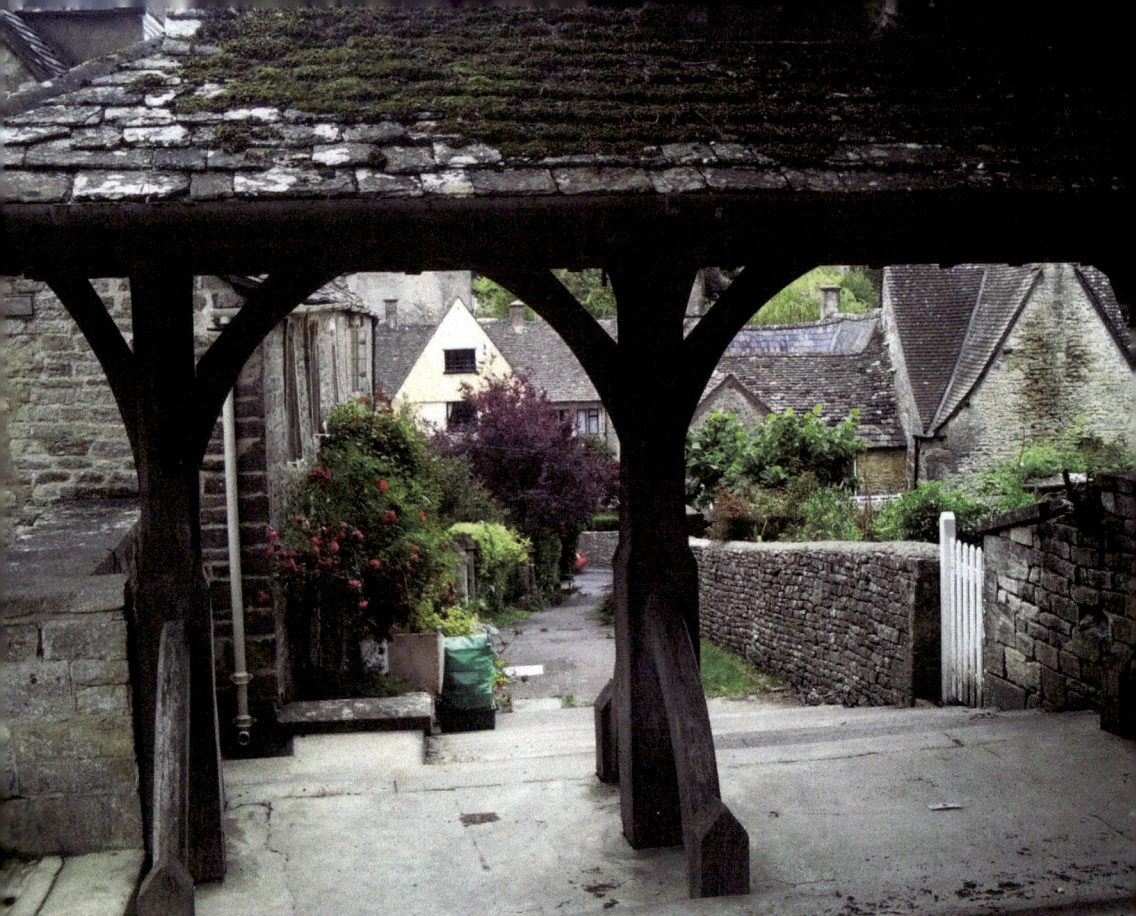

Bisley from the church.

Burford

Burford, which is mentioned in the Domesday Book, has a fine main street of old buildings descending down to the valley of the Windrush. It received a charter in 1087, and was one of the first towns to be given one. Burford did well because of its wool and cloth trade as well as the stone quarries of Taynton and Little Barrington. In the seventeenth century the Strongs of Taynton and Kempsters of Upton, Burford, made a name for themselves in fine craftsmanship following the Great Fire of London, the building of St Paul's Cathedral as well as Blenheim Palace in Oxfordshire.

In Burford itself in the early 1600s there were bitter conflicts with Sir Lawrence Tanfield, who became lord of the manor, over town administration and finances. Indeed he and his wife were known for their greed. His elaborate tomb in Burford church was to reflect his power and wealth. During the turbulence of the Civil War there was an incident when prisoners who were Levellers were locked in the church for disobedience. One 'Antony Sedley' carved his name on the font and 'prisner 1649'. Some were executed by firing squad as examples.

Later on in the century, at the Restoration, Burford recovered and prosperity came to the town because of the Burford Races, considered only second to Newbury, which Charles II attended with Nell Gwynn. One of their children was called the Earl of Burford! It was at this time that saddlery flourished and items were presented to both Charles II and William II. At the end of the seventeenth century and beginning of the eighteenth a growing coaching trade came through the town as it was on the route between Oxford and Gloucester. However, with the building of a bypass and the advent of the railway, although it didn't come to Burford, the town began to stagnate financially and that explains why the character of the town was unbesmirched by Victorian buildings, which later pleased the tourist trade and delighted 'the modern visitor' – once again rescuing Burford from the financial doldrums.

The parish church has a Norman tower topped by a fifteenth-century spire from when wealth from the wool trade was coming into the town, but Victorian restoration was disapproved of justifiably by William Morris, which caused the Revd Cass to remark, 'The church Sir is mine and if I choose to I shall stand on my head in it!'

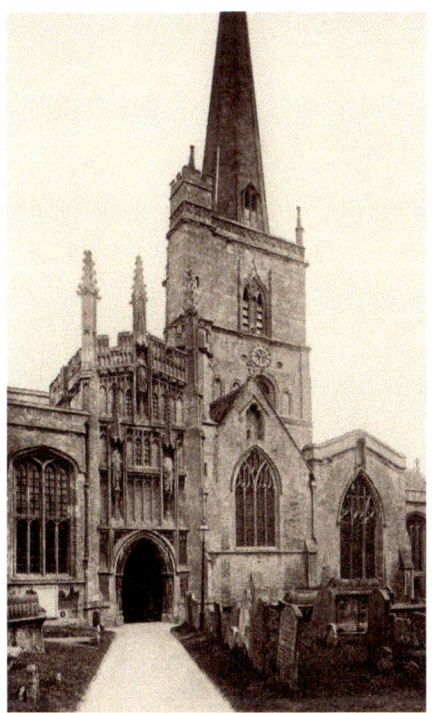 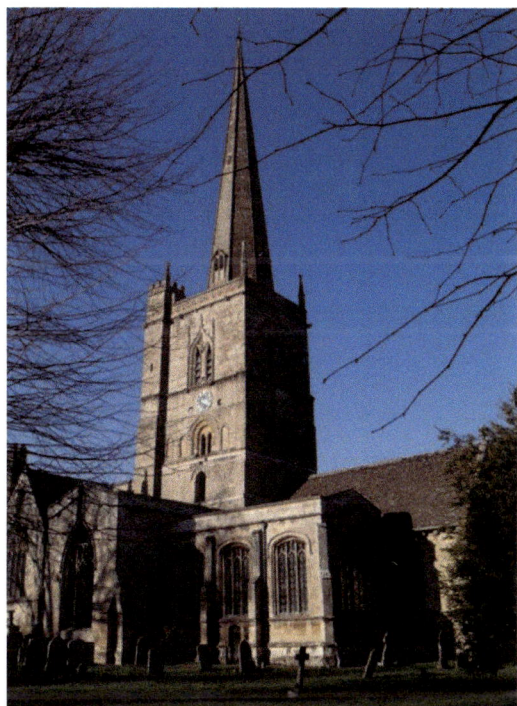

Above left: St John the Baptist Church, Burford.

Above right: Burford church today.

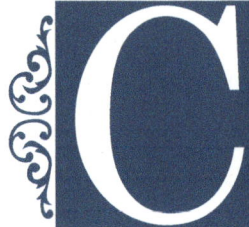

Castle Combe

Nine miles north-west of Malmesbury and 10 miles north-east of Bath lies the Wiltshire village of Castle Combe, which retains its character as a medieval village and has the reputation of being the 'prettiest village in England'. It is nestled in the wooded valley of the By Brook. A site nearby on a hilltop golf course was once a Roman hill fort near to the Fosse Way. It was taken over by the Saxons but was rebuilt as a castle by the Normans in 1135. The Dunstanville family owned the castle following the Norman Conquest and the thirteenth-century tomb of Walter Dunstanville can be found in the parish church.

In the Middle Ages Castle Combe became a foremost wool producer, promoted by the lord of the manor, John Falstolf, who built fifty weavers' cottages and fulling

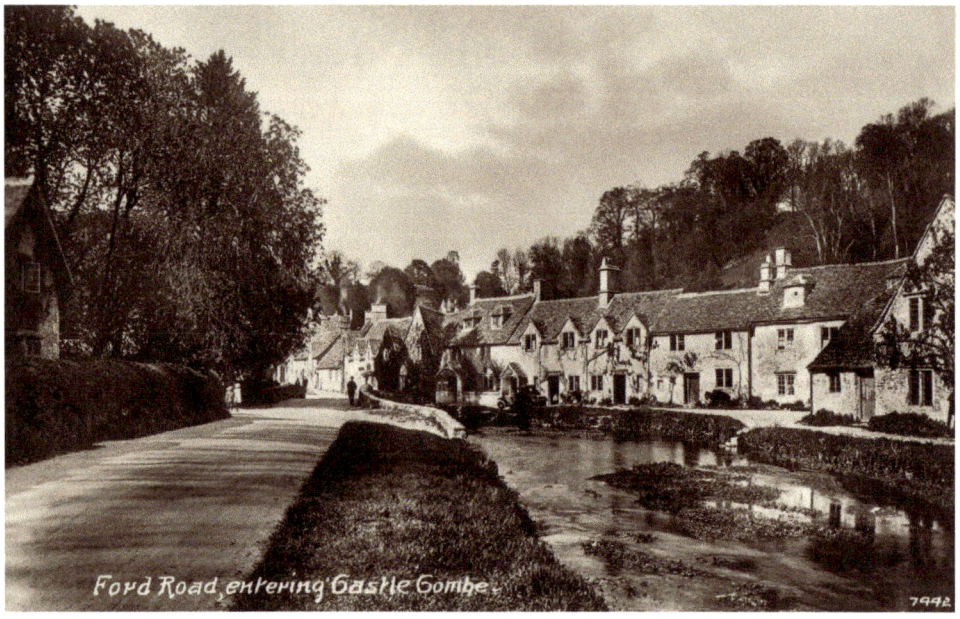

The main street and Bybrook River, Castle Combe.

mills along the river. A red and white cloth known as 'Castlecombe' was supplied to Henry V's troops when fighting at Agincourt in France. There were seventy cloth workers in the fifteenth century and the town had weekly markets and an annual fair around the market cross. Sheep and wool were traded, amongst other things, and John Aubrey is recorded as saying 'the most celebrated faire in North Wiltshire for sheep is at Castle Comb ... whither sheep masters doe come from as far as Northamptonshire'. On the tower of the parish church there are carvings of shears, shuttles and weavers' tools. However in the later seventeenth century the wool industry began to decline because of competition with large industrial centres like Bristol and Gloucester and the little river could not accommodate the new larger machinery. In 1820 the clothing mills and dye houses closed and the medieval character of Castle Combe was preserved – hence its reputation as a good location for films and dramas. However as a nod to the twenty-first century, nearby, on a former Royal Airforce airfield, is the Castle Combe circuit for motor racing.

Cheltenham

Named after the local river, Cheltenham began life as an Anglo-Saxon village. In 1086, the time of the Domesday Book, its population was less than 200. In 1226 it became a market town, which was the basis of its economy until the eighteenth century when medicinal waters were discovered in the town. In the seventeenth century it was foremost an agricultural settlement with a population of around 1,500 but during this time there was a malting industry and a leather industry accounting for the number of tanners, shoemakers and glovers in the area. In the eighteenth century because of pigeons being observed eating calcareous deposits in a field to the south, near to where Cheltenham Ladies' College was to be built, a spring was found with health-giving properties. Between 1738 and 1742 the owner of the spring, Henry Skillicorne, deepened the spring and turned it into a well. He created an avenue of trees leading to the well and he also built the Assembly Rooms where people could play cards and dance. The spa became more popular because a book was written by Dr Short extolling the virtues of taking the waters, but what caused more of a stir was King George III coming to Cheltenham on a five-week visit in 1788. So many visitors were now coming that a search was made for a new well. In 1809 Montpellier Spa, with its magnificent gardens, opened – then Sherborne Spa in 1818 – when the Promenade was laid out as a tree-lined walk, although it was built up just two years later. Pittville Pump Room was built in 1830. In 1801 the population was just over 3,000 but in the nineteenth century the population exploded, reaching 35,000 by 1851.

All sorts of services were now provided for the citizens of Cheltenham. In 1786 a group called the Paving Commissioners set out to pave, clean and light the streets with oil lamps while in 1818 gas lighting was introduced. A private company supplied piped water in 1824 and in 1834 a sewerage company was formed. In 1877 Cheltenham Spa was incorporated, meaning that a mayor and corporation replaced the Paving Commissioners. An electricity supply was brought to the town in 1895. Trams served the streets from 1901 until 1930.

In the nineteenth century spas fell out of favour but Cheltenham remained a popular tourist destination with its array of shops. The railway had arrived in 1840. The art gallery opened in 1899 and the Everyman Theatre just eight years before. The town became renowned for its educational establishments and sport – especially cricket and horse racing, particularly the Gold Cup. Today the population numbers around 110,000. The museum and art gallery is named after Edward Wilson, a son of the town who died on Scott's expedition to Antarctica in 1902. He was an artist and naturalist. When they returned from the first voyage Cheltenham fell in love with 'everything Antarctic' – there were drawings to see and books were published. When the men were lost on the second voyage the town was heartbroken. A statue of Edward Wilson was created by Scott's widow Kathleen, who was a sculptor. It can be found on the Prom near the Neptune Fountain.

The Neptune Fountain, Cheltenham.

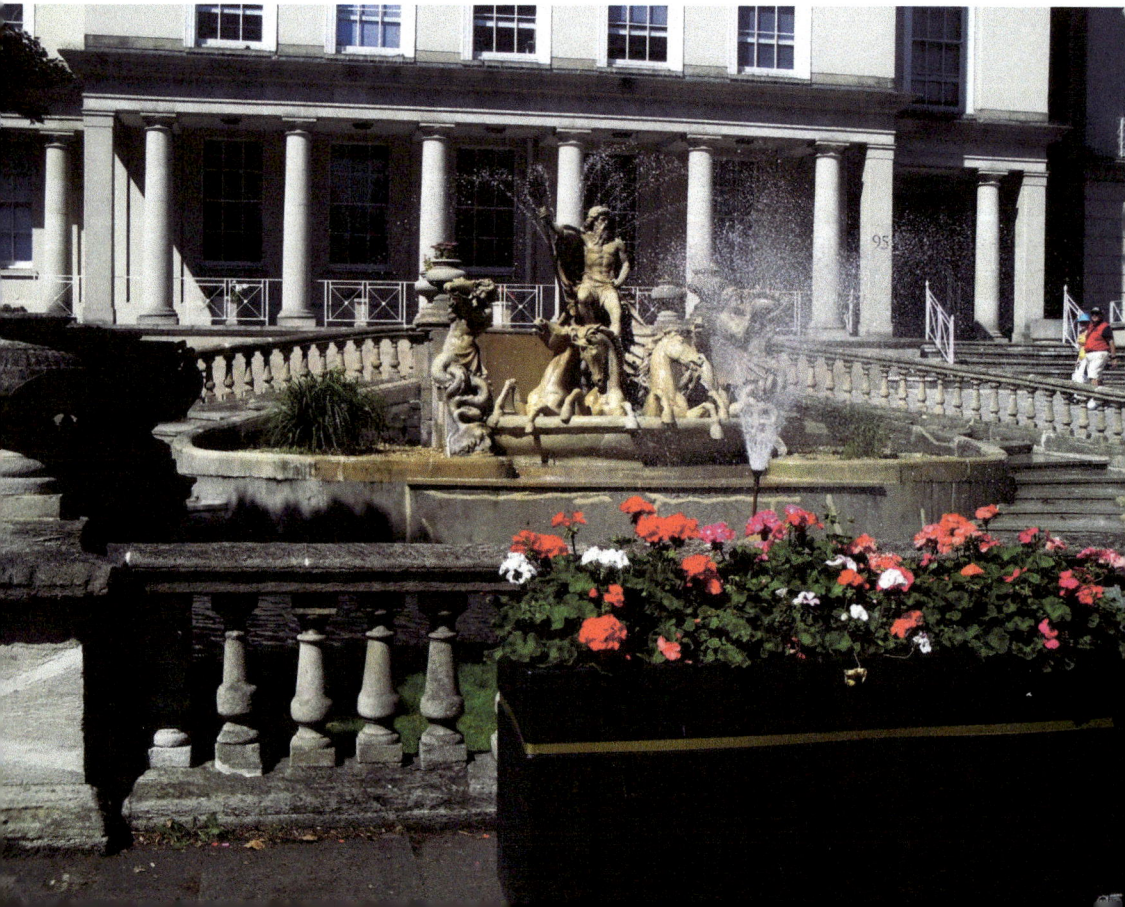

Chipping Campden

The market town of Chipping Campden is one of the jewels of the Cotswolds. Its name dates back to the seventh century as 'camp denu', meaning valley with enclosures. In 1175 Henry II granted a charter for the holding of a weekly market and annual fairs – hence the name 'chipping' was affixed indicating the status of a market. In the Middle Ages it was a flourishing centre for wool with the availability of lustrous fleece from the local Cotswold lion sheep. Chipping Campden's church dates back to the thirteenth century and was financed by the wool trade. Grevel's House was built in 1380 by William Grevel, financier to Richard II. His brass in the church describes him as 'the flower of wool merchants of all England'. Almshouses were built as well as the impressive market building.

In 1902 silversmith C. R. Ashbee arrived in the town with forty cockney families (150 people) from Whitechapel in London, attracted to the area by its tradition of craftsmanship. Here the Guild of Handicraft was formed – including cabinetmakers, wrought-iron manufacturers, blacksmiths, silversmiths, jewellers, enamellers, printers and bookbinders – to be run on the principles advocated by John Ruskin

The seventeenth-century Market Hall, Chipping Campden.

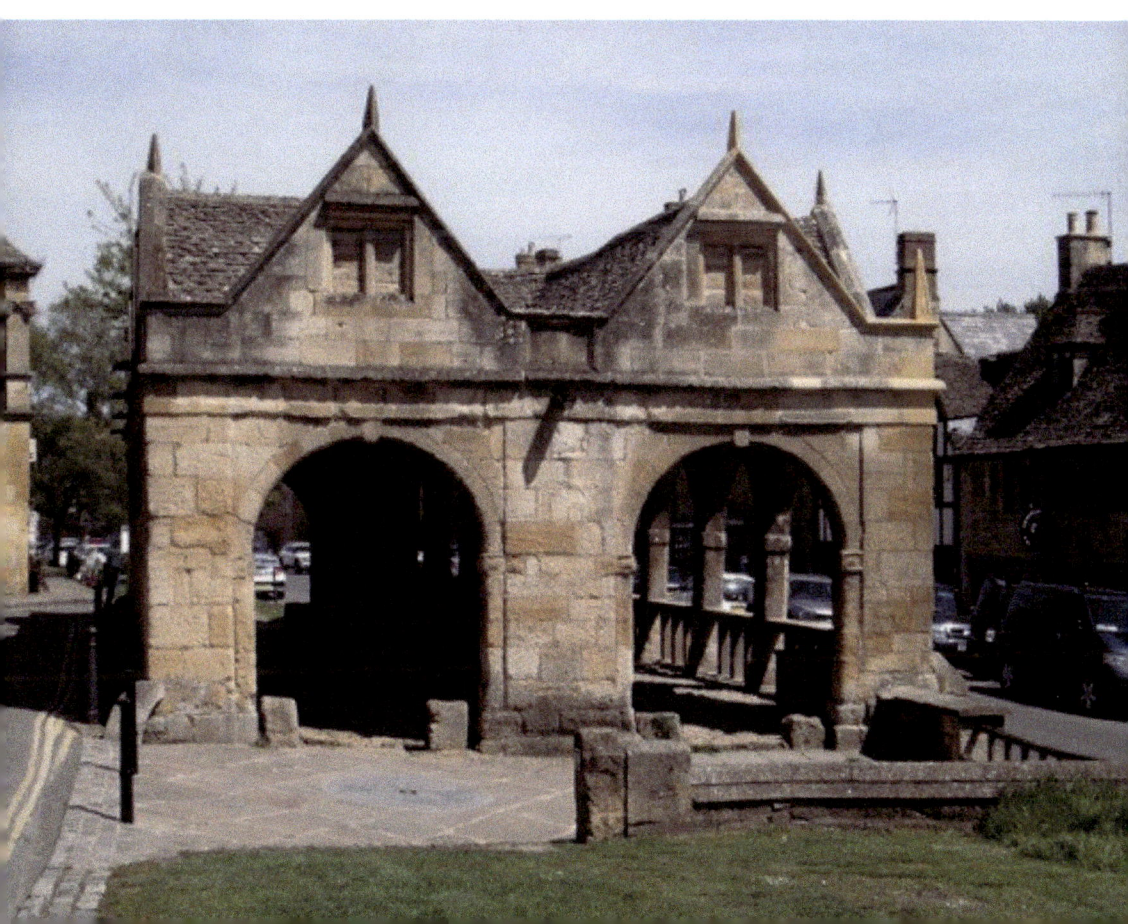

and William Morris, including communal living and profit sharing. Ashbee chose unskilled workers who would adhere closely to the ideals they were taught, and would learn their trade as they went along by the process of manufacture. Machine-wrought items were frowned upon as Ashbee believed that the machine killed the integrity of a piece and that the hand-wrought was far superior.

However by 1910 the experiment was beginning to founder due to the availability and cheapness of machine-made items which looked similar, being at a distance from any commercial outlet and the lack of any outside employment. Ashbee's achievements included the founding of a new Arts and Crafts school at Elm Tree House. He renovated and lived in the Woolstaplers' Hall from 1902 to 1911 and he saved Grevel's House. Craft workshops were run in the Silk Mill and the descendants of the original experiment are still found practising crafts in Chipping Campden to this day.

Near the church is the Court Barn Museum celebrating Ashbee and his fellow craftsmen, with craftsman-made pieces on display. Arts and Crafts ware has never been more popular, with its beauty, honesty and simplicity and its mode of production often obvious from its appearance. Indeed Ashbee's legacy lives on in many places, so his experiment, although short-lived, must be deemed a success in this respect. Chipping Campden is one of those places which deserves a visit not only because of its beauty but because of this heritage.

Cirencester

Cirencester, found 15 miles south-east of Cheltenham, was known as Corinium Dobunnorum (the local tribe were the Dobunni) during the Roman era and it was second only to London in size and importance. It was built at the crossing point of Roman roads the Ermin Way, Akerman Street and Fosse Way. Little of the Roman town survives above ground other than part of the Roman wall near the abbey grounds and a turf-covered amphitheatre. The Corinium Museum displays Roman finds, one of which is a valuable acrostic with a Christian symbol.

In the sixth century the Saxons sacked the town and renamed it Coryn Ceastre – hence its name now. It regained its importance in the Middle Ages, as in Norman times Henry I founded the largest Augustinian abbey in England here, although it did not survive the Dissolution of the Monasteries. The abbot became rector of the fine parish church, which was larger than most cathedrals.

The town became rich because of the wool trade and its prosperous wool markets. Cirencester became known internationally and in the fourteenth century an Italian trader, Francesco Datini, is quoted as saying 'the best wool was in the Cotswolds and the best wool came from Cirencester'. Much money was put into building the parish church of St John in the fifteenth century and the porch, one of the finest in England, was built at this time. It also has an impressive interior with a splendid roof lit by the

C

clerestory windows. The east and west windows have medieval glass. There are some interesting brasses, and a silver-gilt cup owned by Anne Boleyn with her heraldic symbol of a falcon is a treasure belonging to the parish church.

To the west of the town is Cirencester Park consisting of 3,000 acres of parkland created in the eighteenth century by the 1st Earl, Lord Bathurst. He was assisted in his design by his friend the poet Alexander Pope and together they laid out avenues and rides. A folly known as Pope's Seat was built in the grounds. A polo ground often frequented by the royal family and the oldest in the country can be found. Matches are held every Sunday from May to September.

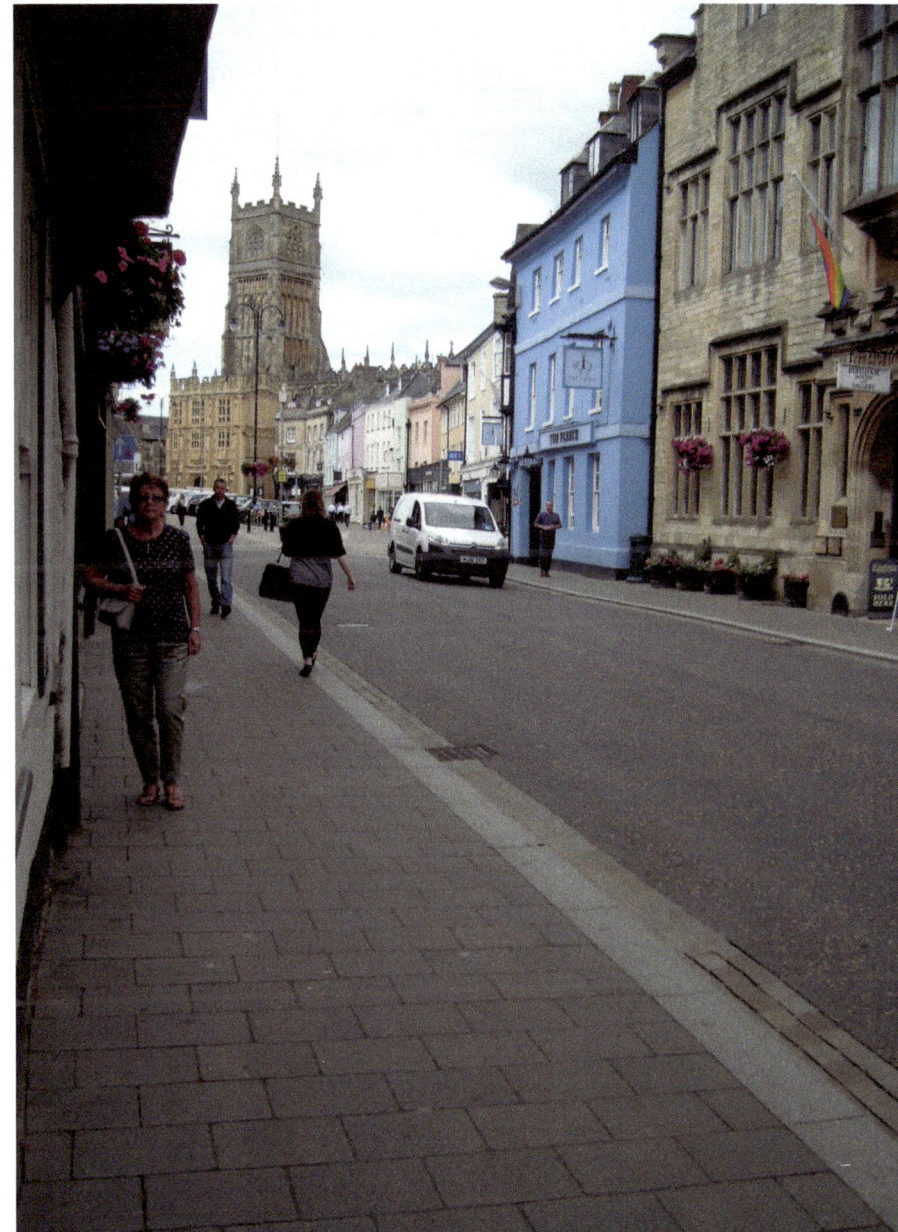

The market square, Cirencester.

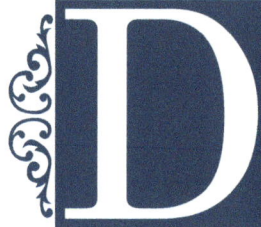

Daglingworth

Found below Duntisbourne Rouse on the River Dunt 3 miles from Cirencester is Daglingworth (the name dates back to 1150 and means enclosure of the family of Daeggel), which has a late eighteenth-century Grade II listed manor house with a magnificent round medieval dovecote with revolving ladder to reach the 500 nesting niches in its curved walls.

To the north are the Church of the Holy Rood and rectory set above the rest of the village. The church is fascinating because, although rebuilt in the fifteenth century and then again in 1840, it dates back to Saxon times. There is part of a Roman altar made into a window by the Saxons with the inscription 'dae matres' – which seems to be a dedication to Junia, the 'genius loci' – a Saxon doorway, plus a Saxon sundial over the fifteenth-century door. This is a square shape with a circular dial with rolled moulding and a central hole for the gnomon. The sundial has been moved from its original position, so the sun no longer reaches it. The most exciting finds, however, are four primitive tenth-century Saxon carvings rediscovered in 1850 as part of the jambs of an arch with the sculpted side inwards. The four are as good a quality as those of York Minster and consist of two crucifixes: Christ in Majesty and St Peter. One of the crucifixes shows a soldier with a spear and a soldier with a sponge soaked in vinegar and the soldiers are depicted smaller than the all-important Christ figure. All these carvings were created by the same talented individual. A fifteenth-century carving of a green man was found hidden in carved foliage on the font. This is a pre-Christian symbol of health and fecundity and is found in churches all over England and elsewhere. It is a symbol which has widespread appeal to our present times with our preoccupation with the environment.

Meanwhile there is an extensive quarry in Gloucester Road being excavated by Hanson Aggregates for Cotswold limestone for road building and brick manufacture. In the quarry office there are all sorts of fossils discovered in the process: there are sea creatures as well as reptiles and even dinosaur footprints dating back around 165 million years. There are many varied experiences to be had on a visit to Daglingworth.

D

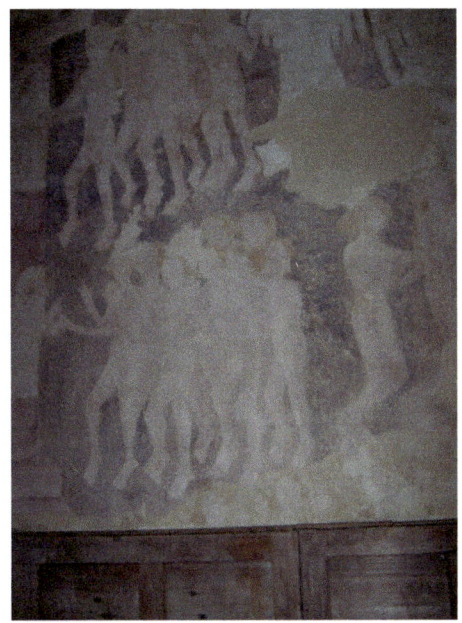 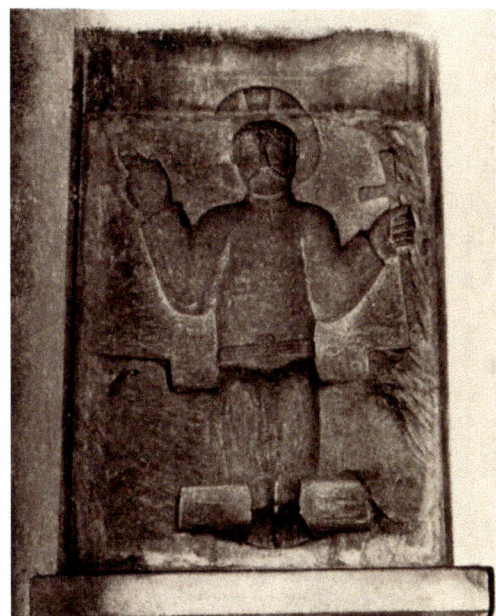

Above left: Daglingworth Doom painting.

Above right: Anglo-Saxon carving.

Deddington

Although there was an eleventh-century motte-and-bailey castle built here by Odo Bishop of Bayeux, it fell into disrepair in the 1200s and was actually demolished in the fourteenth century. It is possible to see grassy ramparts remaining today. But this means that by the time Piers Gaveston, the King's favourite, was held prisoner in Deddington by the Earl of Pembroke only ruins remained. The Earl of Warwick, called the 'Black Cur of Arden' by Gaveston, snatched the prisoner and took him by mule to Warwick Castle where he was beheaded on Blacklow Hill nearby. Thus Piers Gaveston had an ignominious end, showing that being the favourite of a king does not always work in one's favour; in fact quite the opposite.

This ironstone village sits either side of the Banbury to Oxford road just 6 miles south of Banbury. A fifteenth-century Perpendicular church lies between the castle mound and the main road. It has a fine interior and a fourteenth-century brass. Deddington was a market town until the eighteenth century. The Jacobean Kings Arms and eighteenth-century Three Tuns Inn are certainly worth investigating on a visit.

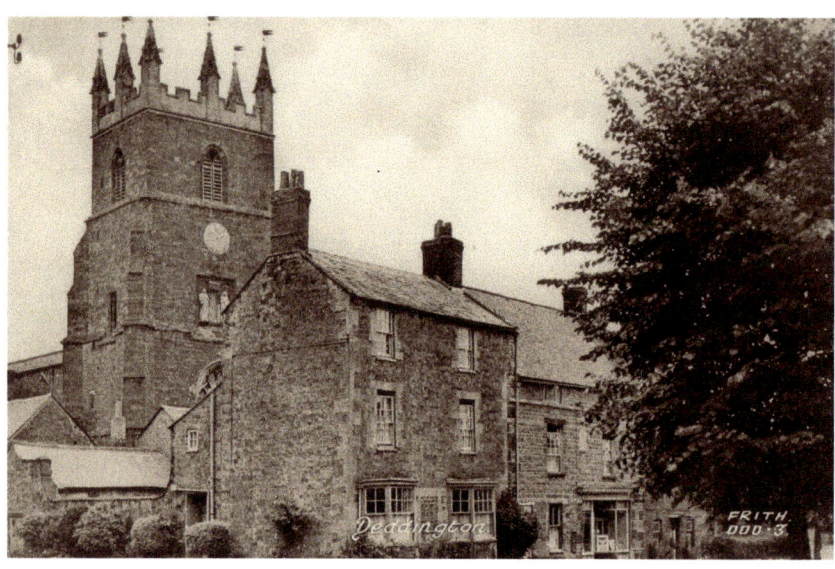

The castle site is in the middle of the town.

Dover's Hill

Dover's Hill, the open grassy plateau above Chipping Campden, is where Robert Dover began his 'olimpick games' in 1604, by extending the 'whitsun games' in reaction to Puritan suppression. The first games were sponsored by Sir Baptist Hicks, a local rich clothier, and Endymion Porter of Aston-sub-Edge, who was 'groom to the bedchamber' of James I and who donated some of the king's old clothes including a ruff, hat and feather for Dover to wear at the grand opening ceremony. On the day traditional sports took place, such as hunting, hare coursing, fighting with cudgels, wrestling, racing, dancing, sword fighting, standing on the hands and shin-kicking. It was so successful it became an annual event and a book of poetry was produced some twenty years later celebrating 'Dover's Games'. A woodcut shows Robert Dover opening the ceremony sitting astride a white horse in his finery with a mock castle and cannon in the background.

The games continued into the nineteenth century after a hiatus during the Civil War. In 1851, 30,000 people poured into Chipping Campden with the idea of 'drinking, brawling and making merry', so the games were closed down to preserve public order. However in 1953, for the Festival of Britain, the games were revived. Despite land enclosure at one stage through an Act of Parliament, the land eventually fell into the hands of the National Trust, so the celebrations were able to continue. If you head that way on the Friday after Whitsun you will be able to witness the spectacle, although the nature of the activities will have changed over the years.

D

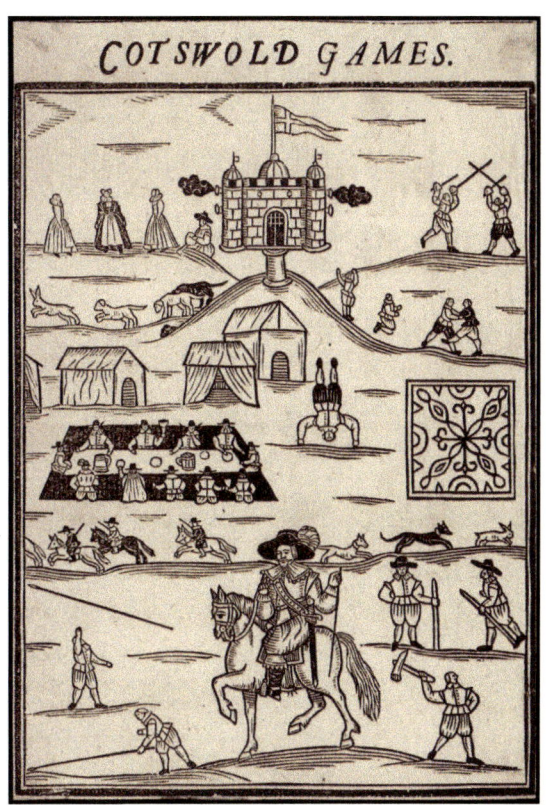

Right: Seventeenth-century woodcut celebrating Dover's Games.

Below: Dover's Hill.

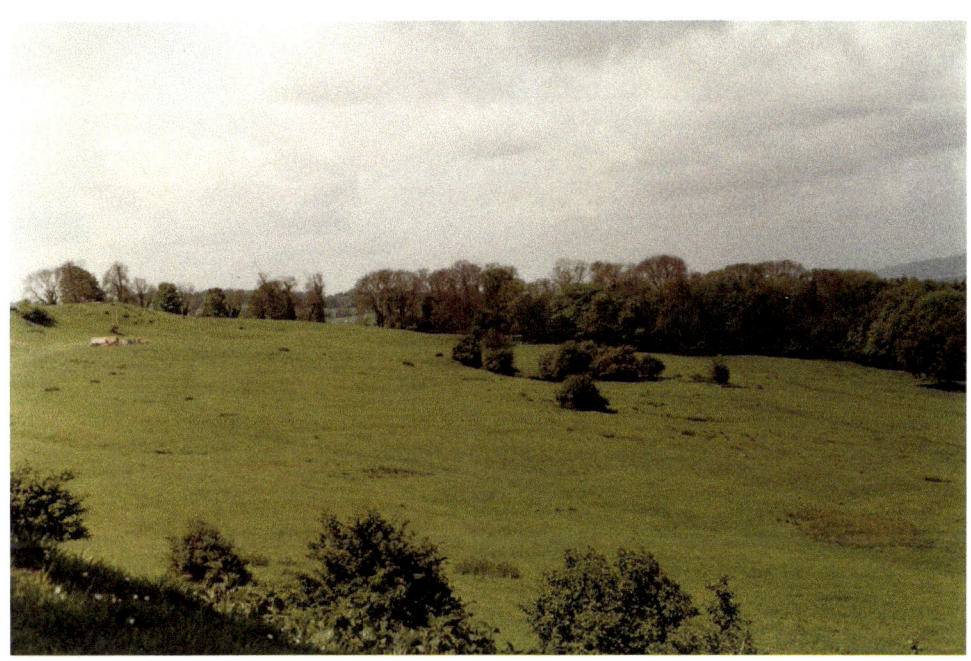

Down Ampney

This village lying 4 miles south-west of Fairford is best known for being the birthplace of the English composer Ralph Vaughan Williams whose father was vicar here. He was born at the Old Vicarage in 1872, which is built from Cotswold stone with brick chimneys, now hidden from view by tall trees – but he only lived here for three years. He named one of his best-known hymn tunes after his birthplace, 'Down Ampney', sung with the words of 'Come Down, O Love Divine'. There is a display about him in the bell tower.

The manor house Down Ampney House and All Saints Church, founded by the Knights Templar in 1265, stand side by side and what is most noticeable about the church is the fourteenth-century spire which is visible from miles around. Down Ampney House is mostly Tudor although it was altered in 1799. The church was partly

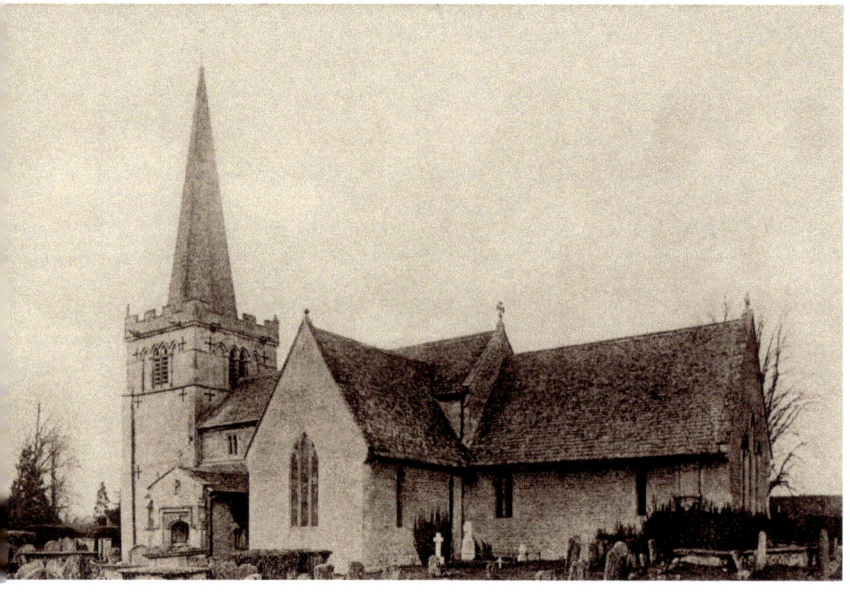

The church, Down Ampney.

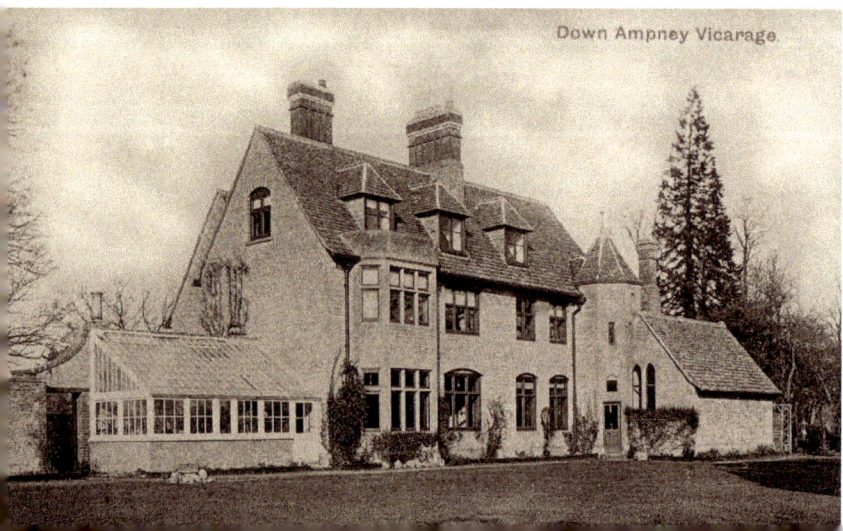

The rectory, Down Ampney.

rebuilt in 1845. A 1637 monument in the church of Sir James Hungerford and his son facing each other over a prayer desk represents the lords of the manor who lived at Down Ampney House. In the south transept are the effigies of Sir Nicholas de Valers (Villiers) in armour and his wife Margaret Bassett who protected the villagers' tools and agricultural implements in a tower in the church – by hiding them. Also beneath the pointed arches in the church are carvings of small flowers painted red which are thought to represent the symptoms of the Black Death.

In the village is a Royal Airforce base whose members were involved with the D-Day landings and the Battle of Arnhem. There is a stained glass in the church with a Dakota aircraft to honour those who died doing their duty.

The Duntisbournes

The Duntisbournes are three delightful villages on the little Dunt stream, outside of Cirencester towards Gloucester.

Duntisbourne Abbots is the most north-westerly and gets its name because it once belonged to the abbots of Gloucester. It is the largest of the three villages. It has an interesting church, St Peter's, dating back to the twelfth century with a low saddleback-roofed tower which is characteristic of the Cirencester area. The lower part of the tower is the oldest part of the church and has a typical narrow window. The tower arch may also be early Norman and the two-bay nave arcade is late Norman. Disappointingly the inside was scraped due to insensitive Victorian restoration while the chancel has been restored since the Second World War and is painted white. The goblet-shaped font with foliar decoration is late Norman, and a Norman piscina protrudes from the south window. There is a worn stone coffin dating from the thirteenth or fourteenth century in the church. It was removed from the churchyard wall to the inside of the church for its preservation.

There are some attractive buildings in the village, and on the old Roman road known as Ermine Street (the old Gloucester road) is a seventeenth-century, Grade II listed building which was an old coaching inn known as the Five Alls. Recently it became unviable. A mile to the south is the Hoar Stone long barrow.

Walking along the course of the Wet Lane from Duntisbourne Abbots you come next to Duntisbourne Leer. Its unusual name comes from the Abbey of Lire in Normandy to which the village belonged until 1416 when it was given to Cirencester Abbey. The pretty village is crossed by a ford with a farmhouse and cottages either side of the water. The ford is shallow and clear, almost lapping the doorsteps of these homes. In the eighteenth century fewer pigeons were kept for meat, so dovecotes started to be incorporated into buildings, mostly barns and farm buildings and in this instance on the farmhouse and on Duntisbourne Leer Cottage. This is one is one of the most photographed locations in the Cotswolds as it is very picturesque with no visible trappings of the twenty-first century.

Each of the Duntisbournes is very different in character, although they are all redolent of the past. Next and nearest to Cirencester is Duntisbourne Rouse, where there is another Norman church, St Michael's, but with Saxon origins, in a sloping churchyard which accounts for the crypt under the church. Duntisbourne Rouse literally means 'the stream of a man called Dunt', while the 'Rous' part is the Norman name of a lord of the manor. It has the local saddleback roof to its tower like Duntisbourne Abbots' church but this interior is fascinating: there are medieval paintings on the chancel wall, eighteenth-century box pews, stalls in the chancel with five misericords which are thought to come from Cirencester Abbey and the church also has an octagonal Norman font. There are twelfth-century windows throughout. It was designated a Grade I listed building in 1958.

The Duntisbournes are peaceful old English villages and to visit them on a late summer's day when the swallows are gathering twittering on the telegraph wires is absolute perfection.

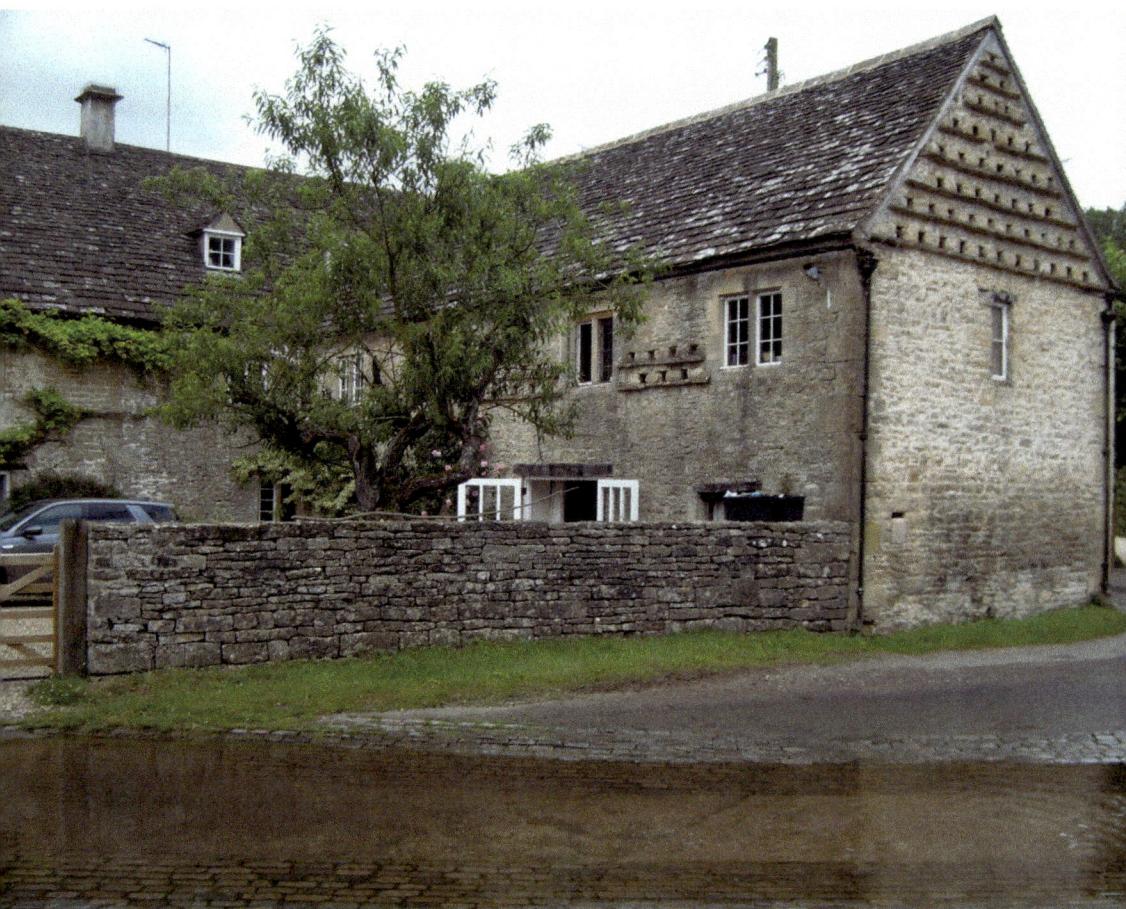

Farmhouse with dovecote, Duntisbourne Leer.

Eastleach Martin and Eastleach Turville

These two villages, 4 miles from Lechlade, with their attractive Norman churches are across the River Leach from each other and were once separate manors, but since 1930 they have been classed together.

The church of St Michael and St Martin, after which the village is named, is no longer used for worship. It is early Norman, having been founded by Richard Fitzpons, and was given to Great Malvern Priory in 1120 and then to Gloucester Abbey. The church is mostly thirteenth century. Eastleach House is nearby. It is a Grade II listed building designed by the architect Walter Cave and built in 1900. It has a formal garden and large grounds open to the public. Eastleach Turville's church of St Andrew is now the parish church of the larger village and is Grade I listed. There is a magnificent tympanum of Christ in Majesty carved over the west door. The Early English chancel is beautiful. The thirteenth/fourteenth-century saddleback roof is characteristic of Norman churches in the area.

Although there were only fifty-two inhabitants in 1086, this grew to 400 during the seventeenth and eighteenth centuries. In 1871, when there were around 506 inhabitants, five almshouses were built. In the 1830s the Victoria Inn opened its doors as a public house – since the eighteenth century it had been a private dwelling. Now it is possible to sit outside under an umbrella on a hot day sampling the imaginative menu while taking in the scenery of the wooded valley where a pair of brimstone butterflies flit amongst the trees only to be disturbed by a lone horse rider.

Of noteworthy people choosing to make their home here, Peter Bailey Williams was antiquary and priest at Eastleach Martin in the eighteenth century. In the early nineteenth century John Keble was curate of St Michael and St Martin's. (The clapper bridge was named after him or after a lord of the manor of the same name.) Jona von Ustinov, father of the famous actor Peter Ustinov, was a diplomat and intelligence agent who worked for MI5 during the Nazi regime and died here in 1962. His artist wife, Nadia Benois, continued to live in the village. This was John Betjeman's favourite location in the Cotswolds and who can blame him? Peace envelops you when you step out of your car, with only a woodpecker drumming somewhere nearby and the daffodils blooming down by the river.

A-Z of the Cotswolds

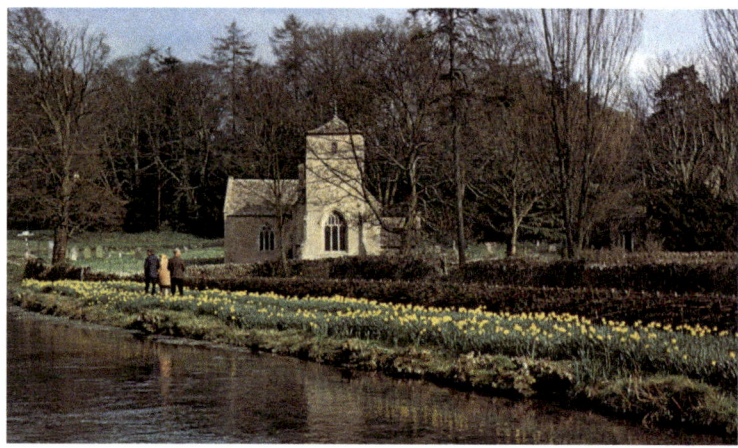

St Michael and St Martin's Church, Eastleach Martin.

Ebrington

Ebrington, located 2 miles from Chipping Campden, known sometimes as 'Yubberton' (there is a local ale taking the old name), is an attractive village of thatched stone cottages, narrow lanes and tiny streets. It overlooks a valley where the little Knee Brook runs to meet the Stour. In the centre of the village is the war memorial and the award-winning pub the Ebrington Arms (with accommodation), wisteria scrambling over its Cotswold stone frontage. On higher ground stands the seventeenth-century manor house and the church of St Eadburgha with its Norman south doorway and geometric design on its tympanum. Inside there are interesting medieval bench ends, a harvest scene on a medieval glass roundel of a sower illustrating October and a seventeenth-century canopied pulpit. Of the monuments there is a seventeenth-century memorial to the respected Keyte family, but especially noteworthy is the one to Sir John Fortescue, Lord Chief Justice, who despite defeat at Tewkesbury in the Wars of the Roses lived to a ripe old age in the village.

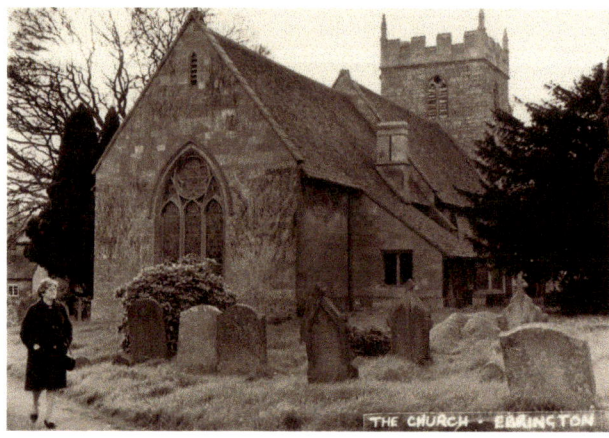

St Eadburgha's Church, Ebrington.

Elkstone

Elkstone, halfway between Cirencester and Cheltenham, was known as Elchestone in the Domesday Book of 1086. The first church was built in 1160 and consisted of just a nave and chancel with a central tower. This tower either collapsed or was dismantled in the thirteenth century.

When re-roofing the chancel the builders raised the walls to form a chamber which was used as a columbarium (dovecote), which is highly unusual in a church building. It is still there to this day, and you can still see the entrance holes in the far wall and the white-painted chamber – sadly no longer home to doves!

Elkstone church has the reputation of being the 'best preserved Norman church in the Cotswolds'. It certainly is the highest in the Cotswolds at 1,000 feet above sea level. It has a fifteenth-century Perpendicular tower with corbel figures and a belfry hung with six bells, the oldest being seventeenth century. There are gargoyles on the embattled parapet and two figures playing musical instruments on the buttresses. The south porch, dating from the fourteenth century, is the treasure of the church. There is a splendid tympanum of Christ in Majesty and there is a gallery of carved stone animals, birds and signs of the zodiac comparable to those at Kilpeck. Inside the church there is marvellous light because of carefully placed windows and an impressive vaulted chancel. There are two 'zigzagged arches' with 'deeply cut chevrons' and the west arch has dragon head stops. Also noteworthy are the box pews and various seventeenth-century fittings. Outside in the churchyard the tabletop tombs are worth investigation.

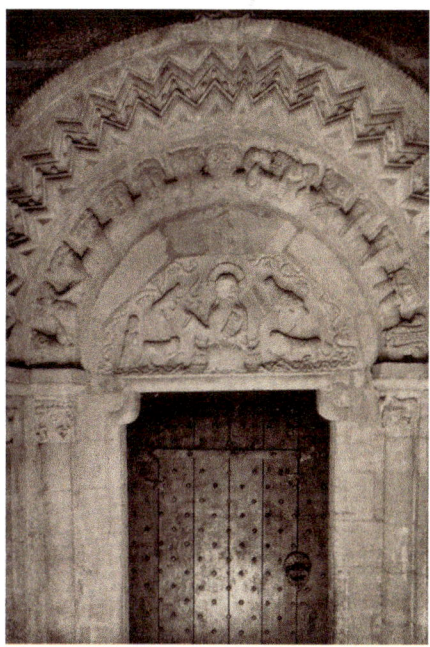

Carved tympanum of St John the Evangelist Church, Elkstone.

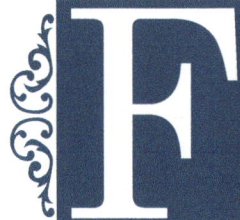

Fairford

Originally a Saxon settlement, Fairford is synonymous with the Tame family who built the magnificent parish church between 1450 and 1550. John Tame and his son Edmund were both wealthy wool merchants who used the finest craftsmen, like the Flemish Bernard Flower who was glazier to Henry VII.

Fairford Church is Perpendicular Gothic and is lit by 'larger windows than previously thought possible with slim stone window mullions and strong buttresses'. In fact the greatest treasures in the church are the twenty-eight windows, dating from around 1500, depicting stories from the Bible, from Adam and Eve to the Last Judgement. They are the only complete set of medieval stained glass in any parish church in Britain. In the chancel are some interesting wooden misericords originating from Cirencester Abbey. Outside in the churchyard it is worth looking for the tomb of Valentine Strong, of the Taynton quarrying family, who died working on Fairford Park in 1662 and the memorial to Tiddles, the church cat which exhausted its nine lives when it fell from the church roof.

When William Cobbett visited in 1826 he amusingly wrote 'one is naturally surprised to see that its windows of beautiful stained glass had the luck to escape not

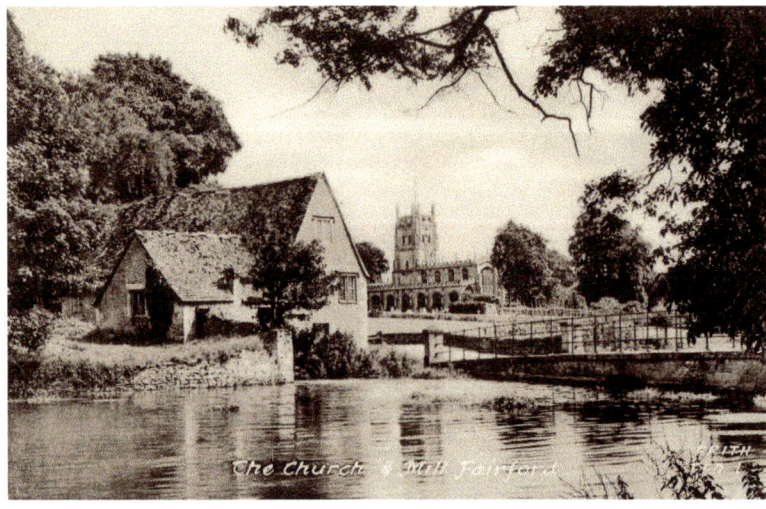

Fairford from the mill building towards the church.

only the fangs of the ferocious "good Queen Bess", not only the unsparing plundering minions of James I; but even the devastating ruffians of Cromwell', and indeed it is wonderful that the windows have remained intact. This was because the windows were dismantled during the Civil War when the Puritans were in the neighbourhood – known for destroying artworks in churches, which to them seemed idolatrous. In the nineteenth century the windows were repaired and re-leaded. During the Second World War the windows were taken down and stored in a cellar for safekeeping. Thus they come down to the present day having survived all dangers for 600 years to be appreciated in the twenty-first century.

Filkins

Filkins is a curious-looking village, as all the cottage gardens have stone slabs edging them. This work was carried out by Sir Stafford Cripps' estate foreman and ex-quarryman George Swinford.

There is a Swinford Museum, unfortunately infrequently open, displaying a good collection of domestic, craft, agricultural and trade tools. Nearby is the finest asset of the village – the Cotswold Woollen Weavers, now in a lovely stone building, producing fine-patterned woollen blankets on traditional weaving equipment. There is a disclaimer that when these looms wear out nobody now produces the equipment, so production will cease. However there is an exhibition about wool and sheep as well as Cotswold weaving. Here you will find a coffee shop and art gallery when you have bought your woollen goods in the main shop. The villages of Filkins and Broughton Poggs run into each other and their churches could not be more dissimilar. Broughton Poggs' church is Norman with a saddleback tower and two Norman doorways as well as a Norman chancel and font inside. By contrast Filkins' church is Victorian French Gothic designed by architect G. E. Street, who also worked on the London Law Courts.

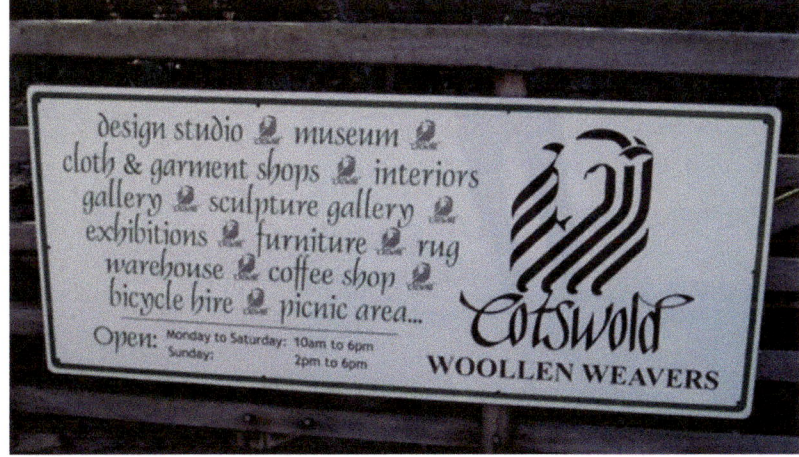

Cotswold Woollen Weavers.

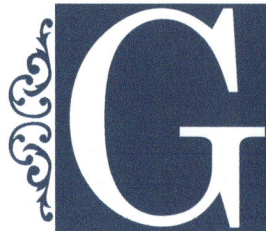

Gloucester

Gloucester is located west of the Cotswold escarpment. In AD 43 the Romans invaded and found this site at the end of the Ermin Way which seemed a suitable site for a fort for the Second Legion (now Kingsholm). Seventeen years later an even bigger fort was built on what is now the city centre. In the Roman period Gloucester became known as Glevum. When the legions moved on Glevum was turned into a town for retired soldiers, but in AD 407 the Roman army left Britain for good and towns went into a bad decline.

After the Battle of Dyrham the Anglo-Saxons took Gloucester in 577 and by 680 the town was reviving. The Mercian King Osric founded an abbey dedicated to St Peter where the cathedral is now. In the tenth century Gloucester was an important centre for Mercia, so Queen Aethelflaed, daughter of Alfred the Great, replanned and fortified the town as a defence against invading Danes. It was during this time that Gloucester took on the appearance we would recognise now with Northgate, Westgate, Southgate and Eastgate all meeting at a central point. Gloucester became capital of its own shire in Saxon times. Aethelflaed founded the new Minster Church of Saint Oswald in 900 when the seventh-century king and saint's bones were interred there and it became an important shrine. Gloucester became one of the three most important cities, equal to Winchester and London, during Edward the Confessor's reign and the king held yearly meetings here with his Great Council. This tradition was continued by William the Conqueror and it was here that the Domesday Book was planned and agreed upon.

In 1216 Henry III was crowned at St Peter's Abbey and permitted oak trees to be taken from the Forest of Dean for the building of Greyfriars (Franciscan friars) and Blackfriars (Dominican friars). Abbot Thokey accepted the body of Edward II in 1327 to be buried in St Peter's Abbey, which in turn attracted pilgrims and wealth to the city. The investment in the abbey meant that by 1470 it resembled the cathedral we know today.

In 1500 the glamorous Fleece Hotel was built, still standing today, and in 1541 Gloucester was given its own bishop and the abbey church was made into a cathedral. In the reign of 'Bloody Queen Mary', who was Catholic, John Hooper, a Protestant bishop, was martyred in front of his cathedral by being burnt at the stake for being a heretic in 1555. Throughout the later years of the sixteenth century and lastly in 1637 there were various outbreaks of plague in Gloucester. Elizabeth granted port status to the city, opening up trade links. In the seventeenth century, during the Civil War, the Parliamentarian city of Gloucester was besieged by the Royalists, who outnumbered them twenty to one. The siege lasted for twenty-six days and finally ended on 5 September – now celebrated as Gloucester Day!

During the nineteenth century the city became an industrial success with iron ore, coal and timber available from the Forest of Dean. Gloucester was famed for pin-making and bell founding. The Sunday school movement started here, as did prison reform. The Gloucester and Sharpness Canal brought growth to the timber industry, and the dry docks and warehouses grew. The railway brought prosperity and the population grew sixfold. In the twentieth century industry expanded, embracing aircraft production, railway rolling stock, motorbikes and, by contrast, matches. There was a regeneration of the dock area and Gloucester continues to attract investment into the twenty-first century.

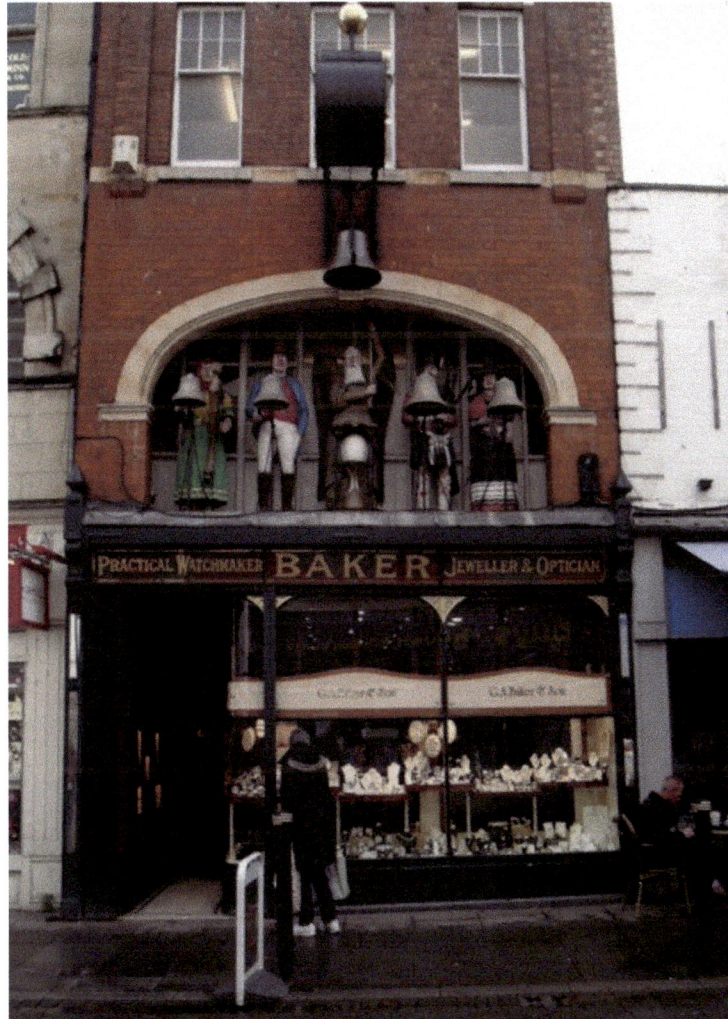

Quarter jacks near the cross, Gloucester.

Guiting Power

A sloping green leads into this attractive village of stone buildings – cottages, the shop and inn. The church of St Michael and All Angels has Norman origins and is Grade II listed, and incidentally there is a hymn tune called 'Guiting Power' by John Barnard for the hymn 'Christ Triumphant, Ever Reigning'. Both the Farmers Arms in the centre of the village and the Hollow Bottom Inn on the Winchcombe road are certainly worth a visit and afterwards a stroll might be in order as there is good walking country nearby in the form of Guiting Woods, an extensive woodland area beside the Castlett stream. There is a 14-mile-long footpath from Bourton-on-the-Water which crosses the Slaughters before reaching Guiting Power, and for those interested in natural history there is a 17-acre wetland nature reserve.

Guiting Power has been a settlement since 780 when it was known as 'Guiting Broc'. Archaeological excavation found evidence of Iron Age activity, a Roman figurine and a Saxon sarcophagus and there are the foundations of a Saxon/Norman chapel to be seen above ground, as well as a large kerbed round barrow. The village was part of a manor owned by King Edward the Confessor; more recently it has belonged to John Walker, then Raymond Cochrane, who formed the Guiting Manor Amenity Trust which manages it now. The Trust runs the farming community, renting to Guiting Manor Farms Ltd for sustainable food production which specialises in crops and sheep.

Nearby is Adam Henson's privately owned tourist attraction the Cotswold Farm Park, with fifty breeds of farm animals. He is particularly interested in preserving rare breeds as well as local breeds, like his father before him, and there are examples to be seen on the farm park, such as Gloucester cattle, Gloucester old spot pigs and Khaki Campbell ducks.

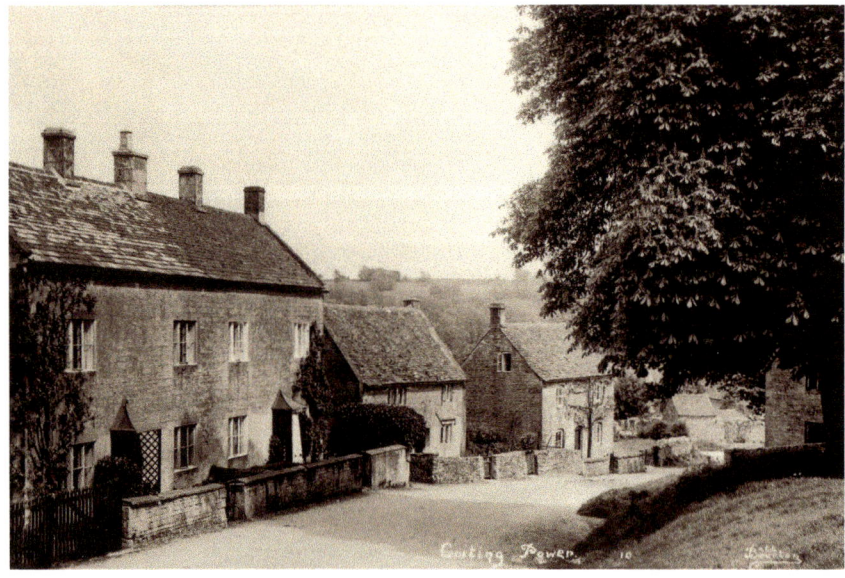

Guiting Power village.

H

Hailes Abbey

Two miles north-east of Winchcombe is the site of Hailes Abbey, the ruins of a Cistercian abbey founded by Richard, Earl of Cornwall, in 1246. He wanted to give thanks to God for saving his life in a shipwreck off the Isles of Scilly. Richard had been granted the manor of Hailes by his brother King Henry III and the abbey was built in its entirety in 1277, then was consecrated in a ceremony attended by the King and Queen and fifteen bishops. Finally monks moved in from a Cistercian monastery at Beaulieu in Hampshire which had been founded by Richard's father. Richard's son Edmund had bought a relic – a phial of the 'Holy Blood' – in Germany in 1270 which had been authenticated by the

The fifteenth-century abbey at Hailes.

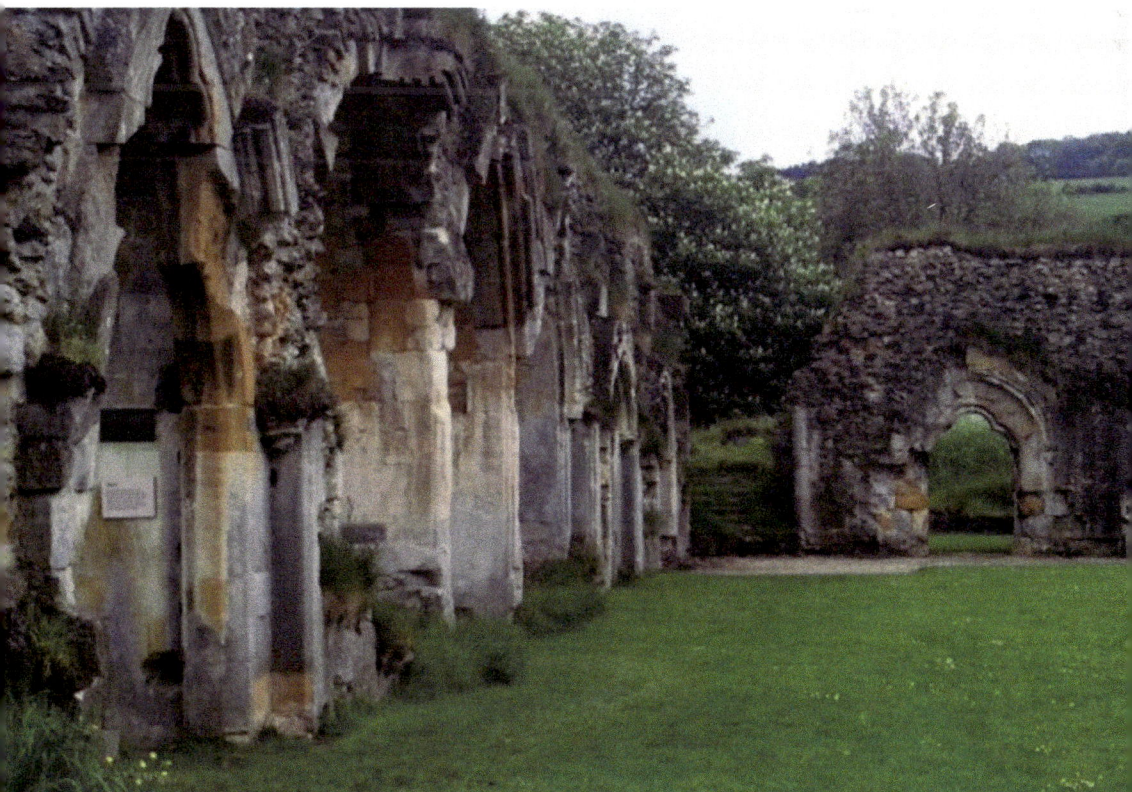

Pope. This he gave to Hailes Abbey and it became a great attraction for pilgrims and attracted so much money that the abbey was able to be rebuilt quite lavishly.

However things were not to carry on so rosily, as in the sixteenth century came the Dissolution of the Monasteries, and although Hailes was one of the last to submit to the King's commissioners in 1536, it was finally handed over on Christmas Eve 1539. The commissioners declared that the relic was a fake made from the blood of a duck and when eventually a proper investigation was carried out, it was found to be honey coloured with saffron!

After the Dissolution some of the abbot's apartments were made into a house where the Tracy family resided in the seventeenth century. Even these were eventually demolished so that now only a few arches remain with some outlines of building in the grass. The abbey belongs to the National Trust but is managed by English Heritage. It is a very peaceful and picturesque site, particularly when the chestnut trees and Queen Anne's lace are in flower and at their best. There is a small museum where various finds are on display besides roof bosses and tiles, and the story of the abbey is told. There are heritage gifts for sale. But before leaving there is Hailes church to view, which pre-dates the abbey and has some fascinating unrestored medieval wall paintings.

Hetty Pegler's Tump

This Neolithic chambered long barrow can be found in a field 1 mile north of Uley, outside of Dursley. It was built in 3700 BC and is 180 feet long with drystone walls and a central passage of stone containing three burial chambers. It is one of the most

The Neolithic Hetty Pegler's Tump, Uley.

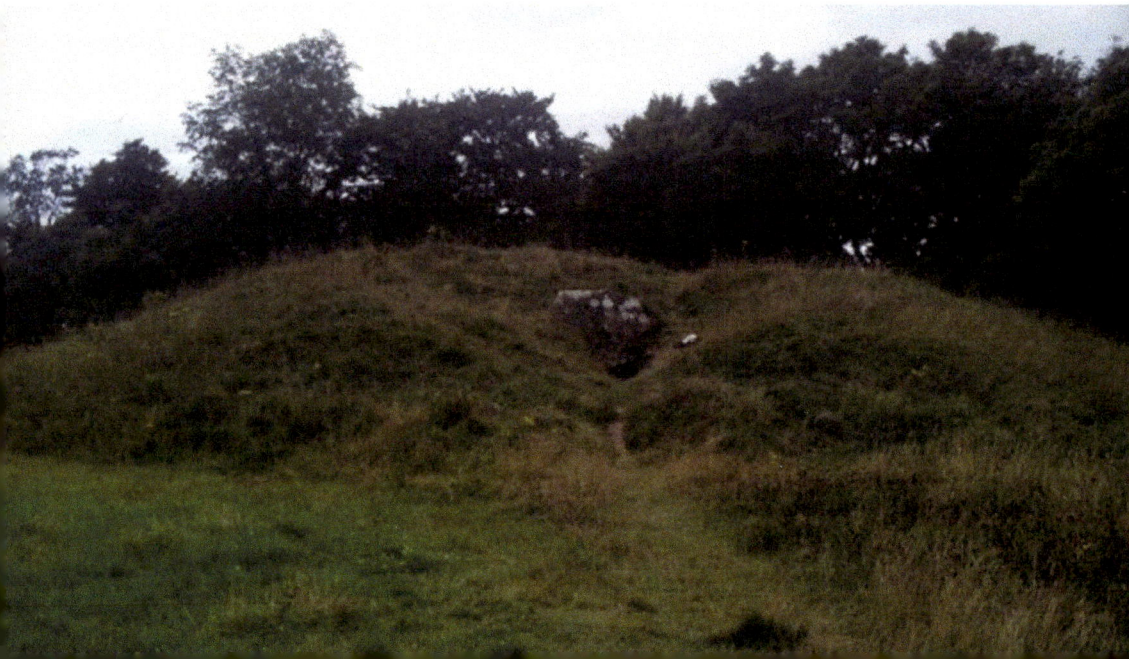

complete long barrows in this country. It would have been for the chief and his family and although fifteen skeletons were found, it may have held twenty-five burials. It may have been named after Hesther Pegler who died in 1694, and there is a tablet naming her in Uley church tower. There is a local story that Hetty came from Uley and used to meet with her lover at the Tump.

Hidcote

The justly famous Arts and Crafts gardens of Hidcote can be found near Chipping Campden in the village of Hidcote Bartrim. The manor was bought by an American, Gertrude Winthrop, in 1907 but it was her son Major Lawrence Johnson who had the idea to make a garden in the fields around the house. He was inspired by Alfred Parsons and Gertrude Jekyll as well as Vita Sackville-West and Harold Nicholson's garden at Sissinghurst. By 1910 he had started work on the main outlines: linked 'rooms' of hedges, shrubs and trees as well as herbaceous borders. He had twelve full-time gardeners employed on the task by 1920. Hidcote's 'rooms' have various themes, for example the 'fuchsia' garden and the 'white' garden, each defined by box hedging,

The garden at Hidcote.

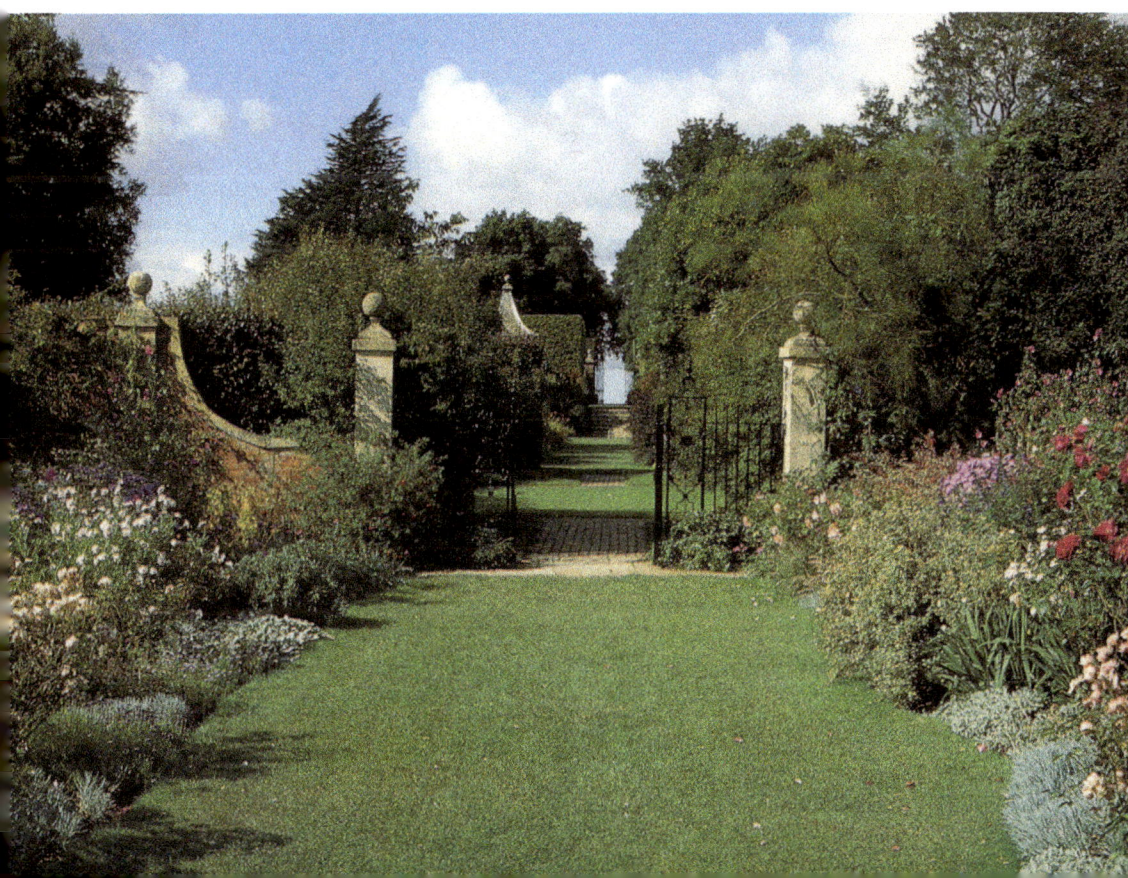

yew, beech or hornbeam or even stone walls, and there are topiaries and fine vistas, or maybe even ponds or fountains. The manor also has outhouses and a kitchen garden. Johnson used the best plants, which have taken the name of the place, like the popular 'lavender Hidcote'.

Hidcote has been widely imitated and is very well known, particularly among the gardening fraternity. It was put into the hands of the National Trust in 1947 when Johnson moved to France ... where he spent his time making another garden!

Horton Court

Horton Court is a Grade I listed stone manor house built in 1521, the manor having been acquired in 1517 by the Revd William Knight, Protonotary to the Holy See and afterwards Bishop of Bath and Wells. He had added the building to a twelfth-century Norman hall there, which still displays some of the 'earliest Renaissance decorative motifs' used in England. It has been in the hands of the National Trust since 1949. The Trust opened the ground floor of the building for some days in 2011 and wants to make it more readily accessible to the public. What is accessible is the 50-foot (15.5 metres) sixteenth-century ambulatory also built by William Knight. Unlike other English ambulatories which are attached to the house, this one is at least 20 yards (18 metres) away and free-standing. William Knight had seen similar ones in Italy and the Italian influence can be seen in the six centred arches but also in the stone medallions of Roman emperors.

William Knight was well-travelled. He studied law in Ferrara when Lucrezia Borgia was duchess there. He was a diplomat for Henry VIII, visiting Spain, Switzerland and the Netherlands in 1527 as private secretary. He petitioned Pope Clement VII for a divorce for Henry from Catherine of Aragon, and although unsuccessful was able to retain Henry's favour to become the king's chaplain. He was even present at the Field of the Cloth of Gold in 1520. He was granted a coat of arms of a double-headed eagle and as he was the Pope's Protonotary Apostolic, a hat with flanking tassels – both these symbols can be seen above the main doorway of Horton Court. He moved to Somerset when he was given two archdeaconries and a canonry in Wells and ended his days as Bishop, being buried in the cathedral.

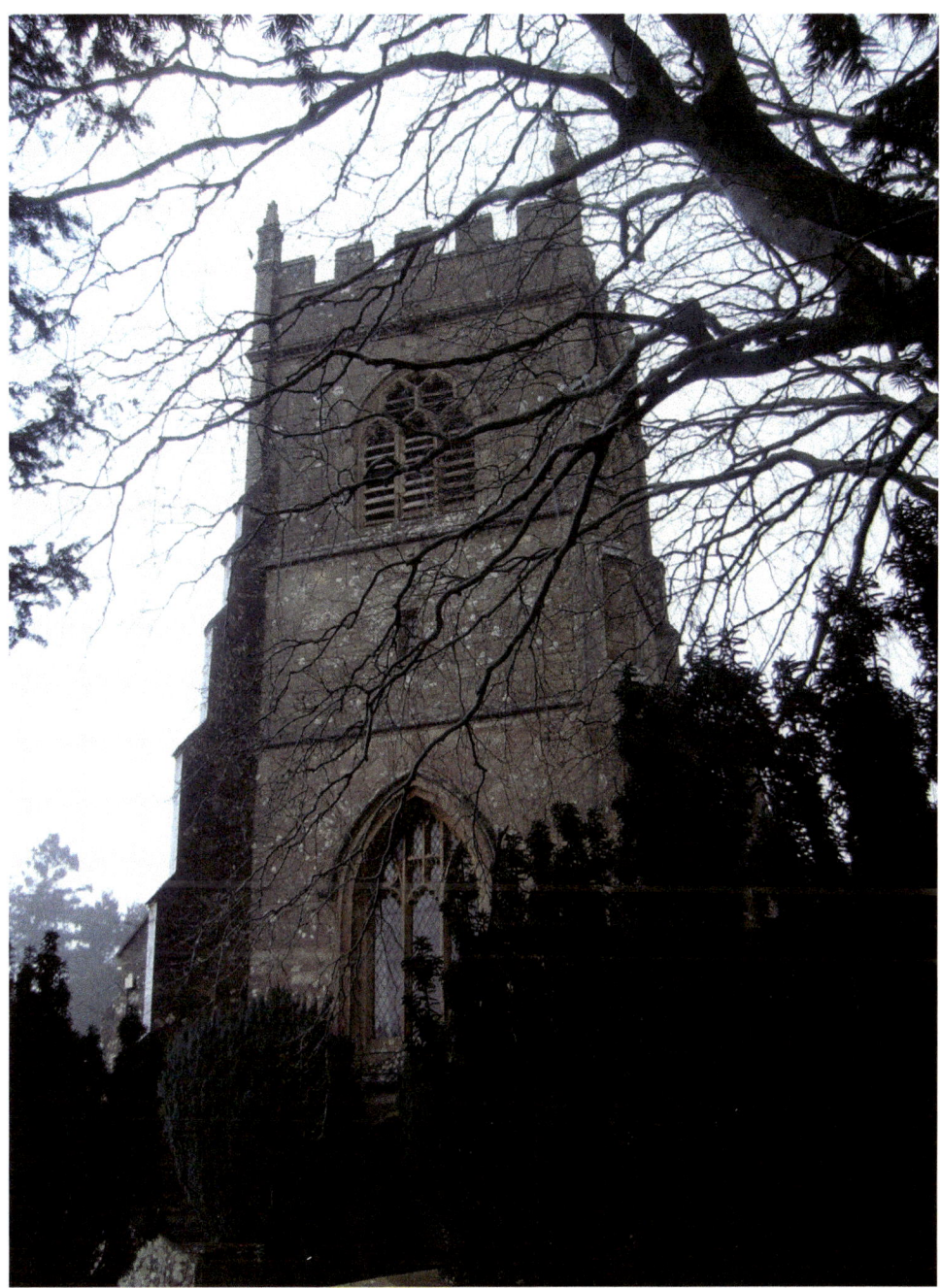

St James the Elder Church, Horton.

Icomb

Icomb once covered 3,000 acres and was a very ancient estate enclosed by Icomb Hill in one direction and Idbury in the other. As King Offa gave part of Icomb to the church in Worcester, Icomb church was in Worcestershire while the rest of Icomb was in Gloucestershire. In 1844 Icomb church became part of Gloucestershire again. Icomb Place was built in the fifteenth century and became the manor house for the whole of Icomb. It belonged to the Blaket family and Sir John Blaket's fifteenth-century tomb is in the church.

Tom, Dick and Harry Dunsdon came from a respectable family in Swinbrook but turned to a life of crime robbing the Oxford to Gloucester coach amongst other evil doings, and fitting circular shoes on their horses' hooves so they could not be followed. They bought a cottage in Icomb where they could stash their ill-gotten gains.

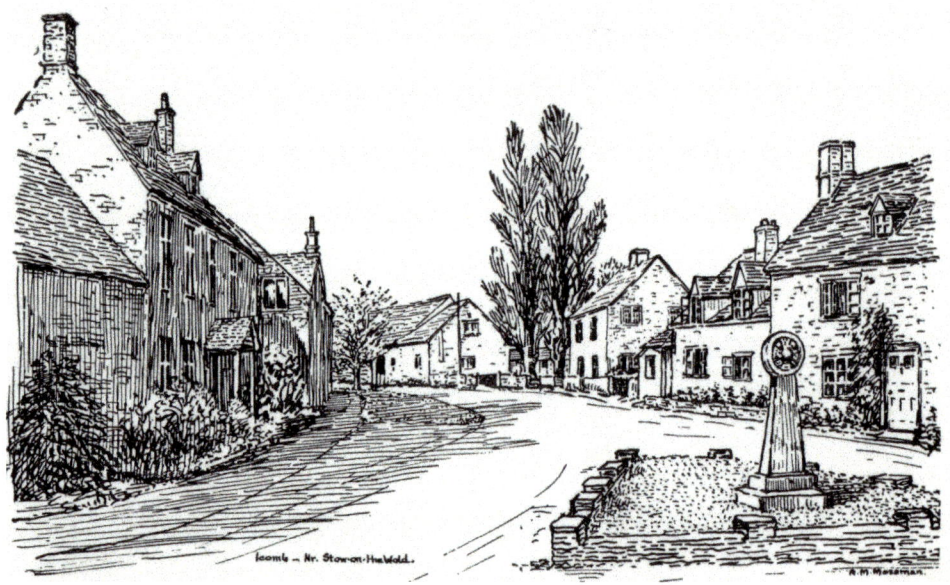

The village of Icomb near Stow-on-the Wold.

I

In 1784 Tom and Harry were caught and brought to justice; their brother Dick had disappeared after his arm was cut off during a robbery – he was assumed to have bled to death. Tom and Harry were hanged on the gallows at Over, and their bodies were later hung in irons on an oak tree at Fulbrook with their initials carved into the bark.

Ilmington

The name Ilmington is from the tenth century, meaning an elm-grown hill. This stone village is located 5 miles north-east of Chipping Campden beneath Windmill Hill and is in the most northerly part of the Cotswolds, and home to Cotswold morris dancing. There are some lovely old stone houses and cottages, darker than the usual Cotswold stone as they are made from ironstone from local quarries, on paths away from the road which runs around the village. The manor house, which has had some sympathetic work done on it, opens its gardens to the public occasionally. Of particular importance is the mostly Norman church dating from the twelfth century which is approached by a field path near two ponds. Its Norman features include the north and south doorways, the windows in the aisle, and chancel arch. Inside is an embroidered map showing the varieties of apple found in local orchards. There is a sixteenth-century porch, oak pews and other 1930s furnishings produced by master craftsman Robert Thompson, also known as the 'mouse man' due to his well-known signature of a carved mouse – and eleven mice are hidden somewhere in the church. (This tradition is carried on in Kilburn, below the moors of North Yorkshire where his descendants have workshops producing sturdy oak furniture.) Also of note in the church is the work of sculptor Sir Richard Westmacott who produced weeping figures and classical urns. He is responsible for a monument to Francis Canning and his wife.

In the middle of the village is a part of a basin used in the eighteenth century to collect water from a chalybeate spring a quarter of a mile to the north-west of the village. The spring was considered to have medicinal properties and aided in the treatment of scrofulous and leprous disorders. Spas were becoming popular around this time, and if fortunes had been different maybe Ilmington might have rivalled Cheltenham or Leamington. Before leaving the village, after all that thirsty work, pay a visit to the Red Lion or The Howard Arms for refreshment.

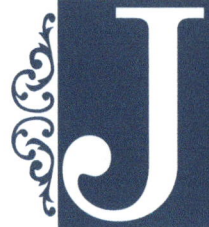

Jurassic Way

Not to be confused with a Northamptonshire footpath of the same name, the Jurassic Way is a prehistoric ridgeway so named by archaeologists, running south-west from the Humber to Salisbury Plain and on to the coast. It follows the high ground on the west-facing escarpment and runs to the hills above Bath in the South West, from the Rollright Stones in the east. It was used by medieval wool traders taking their goods by pack animals to Bristol for export.

Kelmscott

Kelmscott is a village close to the River Thames 2 miles east of Lechlade. The village dates back before Roman times and derived its name in the thirteenth century from 'Coenhelms cort', when there was a settlement of around thirty houses, presumably with elm trees. William Morris – socialist, writer, craftsman, designer – was searching for a rural retreat where he and his family could live in the summer. In 1871 he wrote in a letter: 'I have been looking about for a house for the wife and kids, and whither do you guess my eye has turned now? Kelmscott, a little village about two miles from Radcot Bridge – a heaven on earth; an old stone Elizabethan house – and such a garden!'

Indeed Morris was immediately taken by the 'beautiful grey little hamlet' being 'the loveliest haunt of ancient peace', a building in 'such harmony with its surroundings' that it appeared as if it had 'grown up out of the soil'. It provided a refuge from the ills of the Industrial Revolution and inspiration for his thoughts on rural life. Kelmscott's church, St George's, is twelfth century and there are fourteenth-century wall paintings of scenes from the Book of Genesis. The Elizabethan manor itself was built in 1570 by a farmer, Thomas Turner, and Morris rented it from 1871 until his death in 1896. The house had seventeenth-century Flemish tapestries of biblical stories which must have been appreciated by Morris. After his death the Kelmscott manor estate was purchased by his wife, Janey, when it came up for sale in 1913. It was subsequently passed on through the Morris family, then the University of Oxford, and is now in the hands of the Society of Antiquaries of London. The house holds a large collection of Morris's work – tapestries, wallpaper (notably the lovely Willow Boughs), furnishings, fabrics and paintings including works by Dante Gabriel Rossetti and Burne-Jones. It is now open to be appreciated by the public.

There are some memorial cottages in the village, commissioned by Jane Morris in 1902 to celebrate her husband, and decorated with a carving of Morris by George Jack. A village hall was also built in his name commissioned by his daughter in 1934, designed by Ernest Gimson, and opened by George Bernard Shaw. Morris's tomb in the churchyard was designed by Philip Webb.

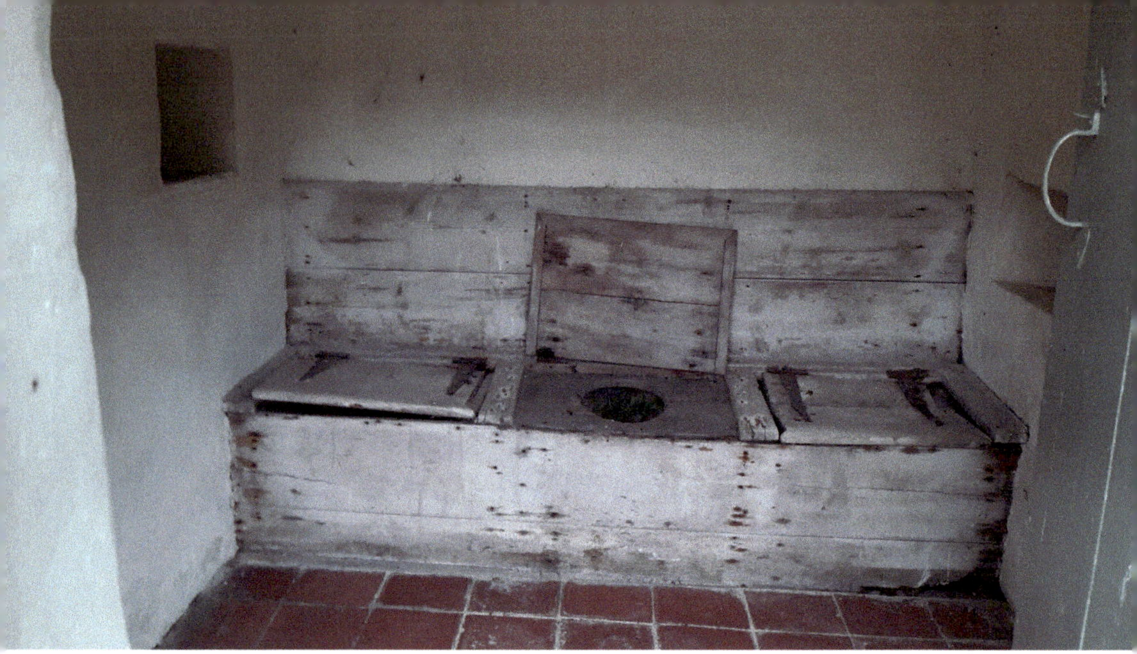

The privy at William Morris's House, Kelmscott.

Kingscote

Kingscote is an attractive village 4 miles north-east of Dursley towards Tetbury, in an elevated position. Its church dates back to the thirteenth century. It has a Perpendicular tower and amongst the interesting monuments in the churchyard is a triangular stone pyramid. A memorial in the church records that in 1788 Catherine Kingscote was married to Dr Jenner of Berkeley. Apparently they had a long and happy marriage and the clever doctor, who rid the world of smallpox by vaccinating with a less virulent strain (cowpox), also cured his wife's depression by treating it with colour therapy – the colour green!

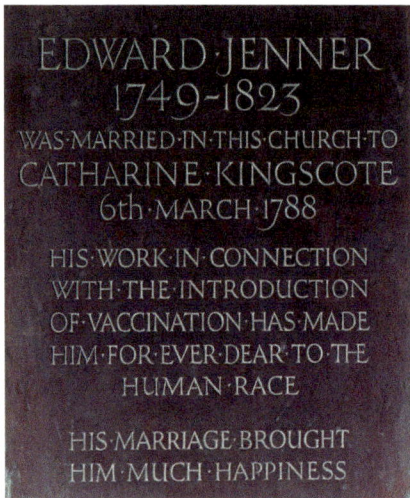

Jenner was following a gas-filled balloon on horseback when he met his future wife.

L

Lechlade

On the southern border of the Cotswolds where the rivers Leach and Coln meet the Thames is Lechlade, home to the highest lock on the Thames, St John's. In 1789 the Thames and Severn Canal opened. The stone quarried in Burford was shipped downriver for buildings in Oxford and London, principally St Paul's Cathedral and Windsor Castle, from Radcot and Lechlade. There are two remarkable bridges: the eighteenth-century Ha'penny Bridge complete with toll house at the south end of the town; and St John's Bridge, dating back to 1228 but rebuilt in the nineteenth century,

St Lawrence Church, Lechlade.

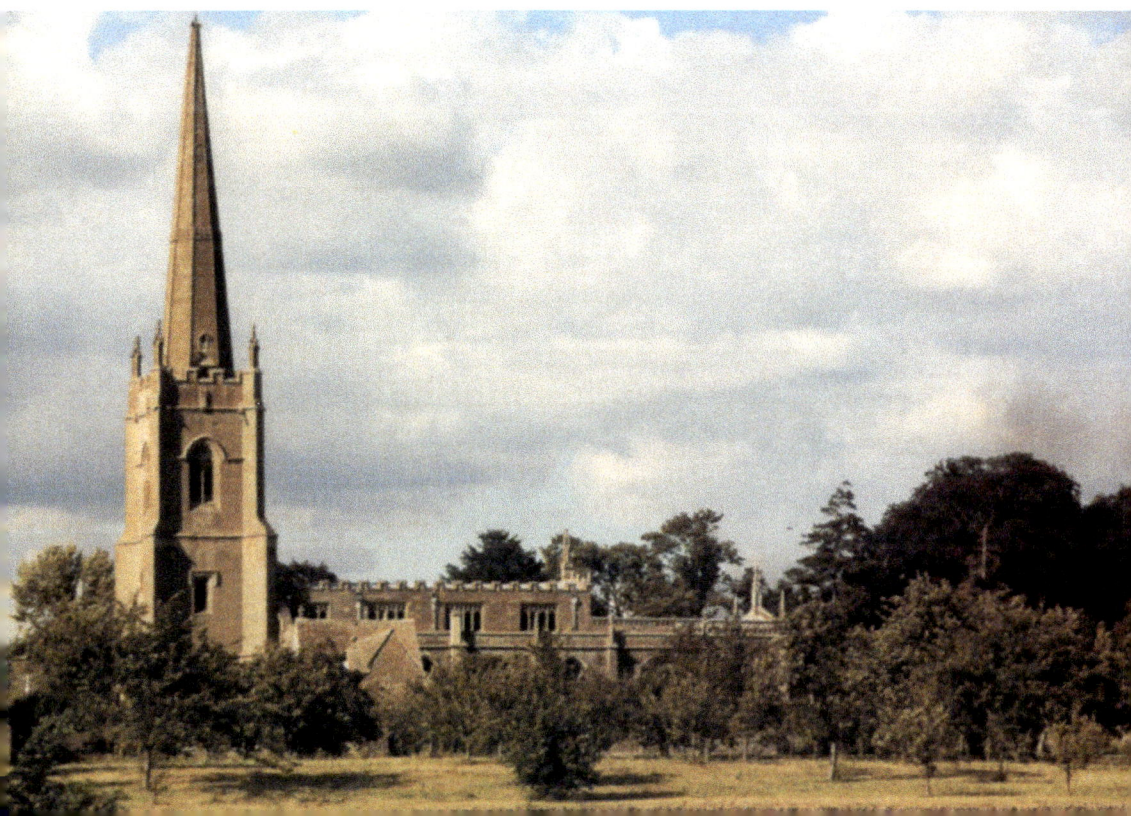

to the south-east in the water meadows. There are pleasure craft on the river now and in the summer these boats moor between the two bridges.

In the middle of Lechlade is a triangular market square with eighteenth- and nineteenth-century buildings surrounding it. The brick New Inn has an 'archway' entrance as it was once a coaching stop. Lechlade's parish church is found here, with its tower housing a fine spire. It is said that it was Lechlade's churchyard that inspired Shelley to write *Summer Evening's Meditation* on a visit in 1815. The statue of *Old Father Thames*, carved in 1790 and created originally for the Great Exhibition of 1851, was originally at Thames Head but now has a home at St John's Lock.

Lower Slaughter

Lower Slaughter is situated 1.5 miles north of Bourton-on-the-Water on the River Eye, which eventually joins up with the River Dikler near Bourton. What is first noticeable about the village is the simple bridges along it and the watermill building with its tall brick chimney which, although looks ancient, was actually built in the nineteenth century and was in use until the 1950s. The name of the village seems to derive from the Old English 'slohtre', meaning a 'muddy place' rather than bloody murders! It's either this or from the Norman landowner Philip de Sloitre who was local to the area.

Although Lower Slaughter is the smaller of the two villages carrying the 'Slaughter' name, it is considered the most beautiful. The manor house, now a hotel, was built by Valentine Strong, the stonemason and quarryman of Lower Barrington and Taynton, in 1650. In the grounds is one of Gloucestershire's largest dovecotes, built in the seventeenth century and now a museum which tells the story of the mill and how it was used in the process of breadmaking. The little River Eye disappears amongst the willows as it leaves the village links Lower and Upper Slaughter.

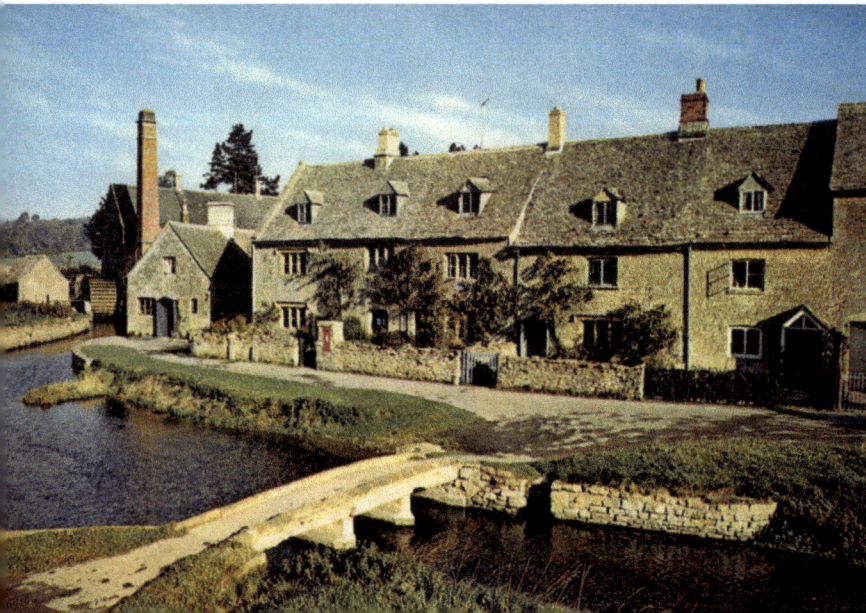

View of Lower Slaughter showing the mill.

M

Malmesbury

Malmesbury is found 5 miles south-east of Tetbury above the Bristol Avon, not far from its source. Although a fine market town, it is best known for its abbey, which was founded in the seventh century and undoubtedly brought wealth to the town. At the Dissolution of the Monasteries it was sold to a clothier called Crump who introduced looms into parts of the building as weaving had become the main source of wealth at that time. The nave and the south of the abbey church became the parish church and in fact we owe much to Crump for preserving the building.

In the fifteenth century a tomb was built here for the body of King Athelstan, grandson of Alfred the Great, which although now empty can still be seen today.

The twelfth-century Benedictine abbey, Malmesbury.

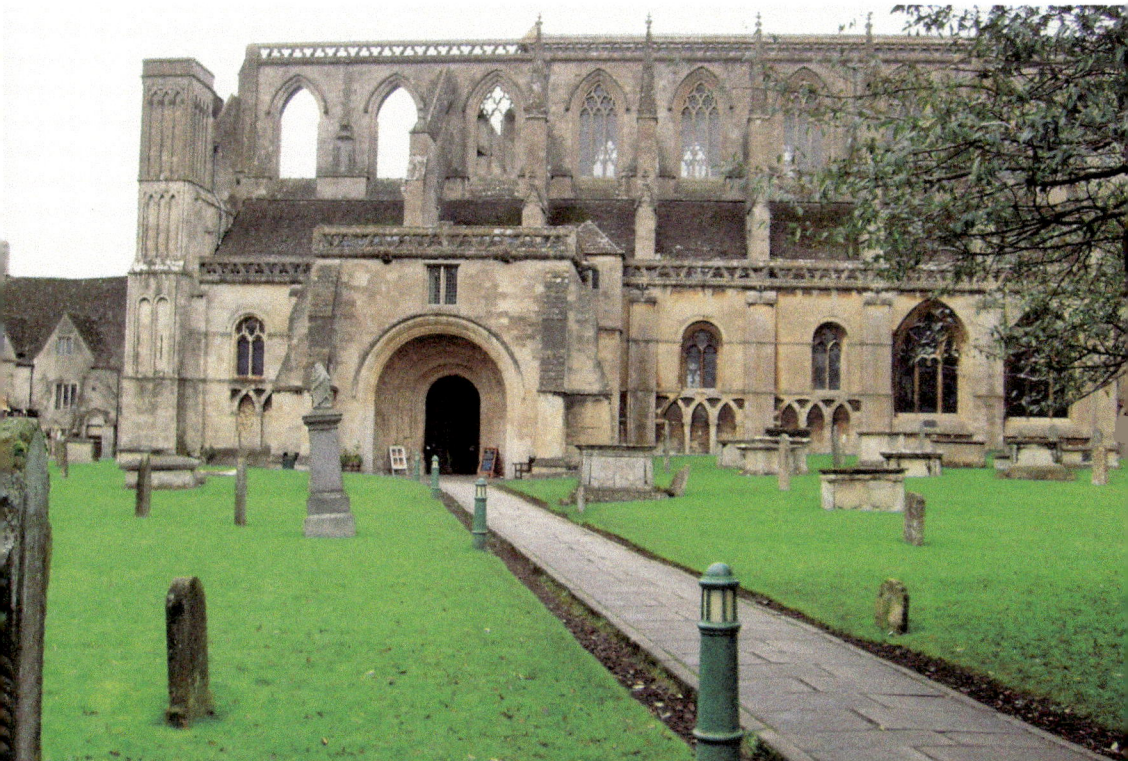

Incredibly, originally there was a spire taller than Salisbury's but unfortunately it collapsed in 1500 and was not rebuilt. The greatest Norman treasure, and one of the finest Romanesque carvings in England, is the Christ in Majesty on the tympanum above the south door with its flanking elongated figures of the Apostles.

Not far from the abbey building is the impressive Perpendicular fifteenth-century market cross 'for poore folkes to stand dry when rayn cometh', as Leyland said, and which is a good introduction to the main part of the town with its mixture of assorted independent shops and seventeenth- and eighteenth-century buildings. Look out for the curiously named pub 'the Smoking Dog', named after a picture of a dog with a pipe in its mouth found in the attic! In the new museum building you can learn about rural life and local industry, such as lace-making. Dyson is a name we associate with the town.

Minster Lovell

The Oxfordshire village of Minster Lovell is in fact 2.5 miles west of Witney but to reach it from the Gloucestershire Cotswolds you approach it through a maze of lanes, arriving at the east end of the village where the church is. The church originally had a priory attached to it – hence the 'minster' part of its name. When it was dissolved in 1414 it was owned by Ivry Abbey in Normandy. The fifteenth-century church is cruciform and has impressive vaulting under its central tower and there is original stained glass and benches. The tomb of the knight Sir William Lovell is worth noting as he was the builder of the church and the manor house, which is found below the church.

Minster Lovell Hall was built in the fifteenth century. It was a fortified manor house, somewhat like a castle, but was dismantled in 1747 and has since become a ruin. But what a picturesque ruin in a peaceful and majestic setting on the tree-lined banks of the Windrush! It was built in a quadrangle with a great hall, kitchens and solar with its circular dovecote now across a stile and an adjacent field. It is said that in the thirteenth century Lord Lovell was defeated in the Lambert Simnel Rising of 1487, so retreated to a secret room in Minster Lovell Hall known only to his servant who was to bring food to his master. However the servant died and the unfortunate lord consequently starved to death. In 1708 repairs were being carried out on the house when the skeletons of a man and his dog were discovered in a secret room, and it is said that when air entered the room the skeletons turned to dust! It is also rumoured that a ne'er-do-well called Freeman was living in the house in lavish style in the 1800s who turned out to be a highwayman responsible for hold-ups on the toll roads of Oxfordshire and the Cotswolds, so ended his days with a noose around his neck. It is true to say that the site of Minster Lovell House is redolent of such stories.

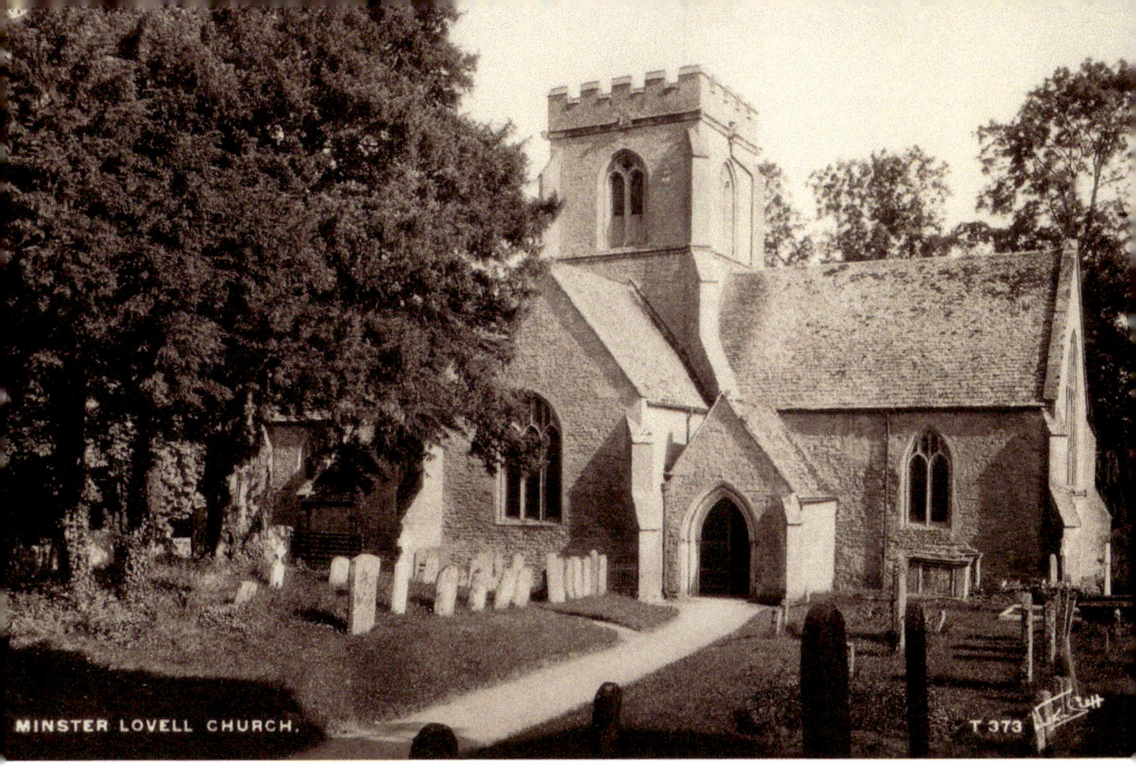

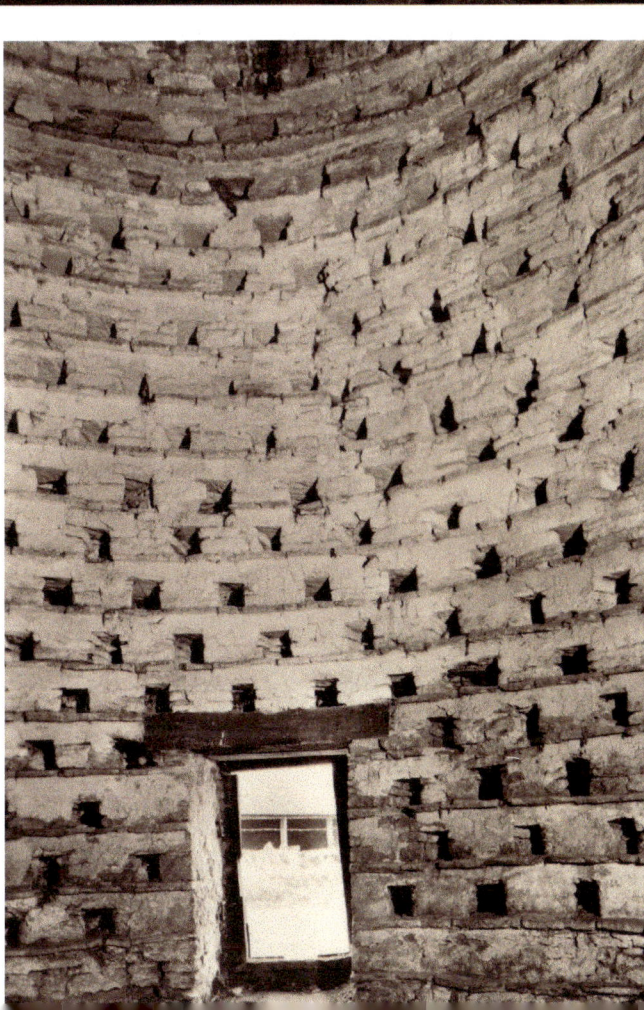

Above: Minster Lovell church.

Right: The dovecote, Minster Lovell.

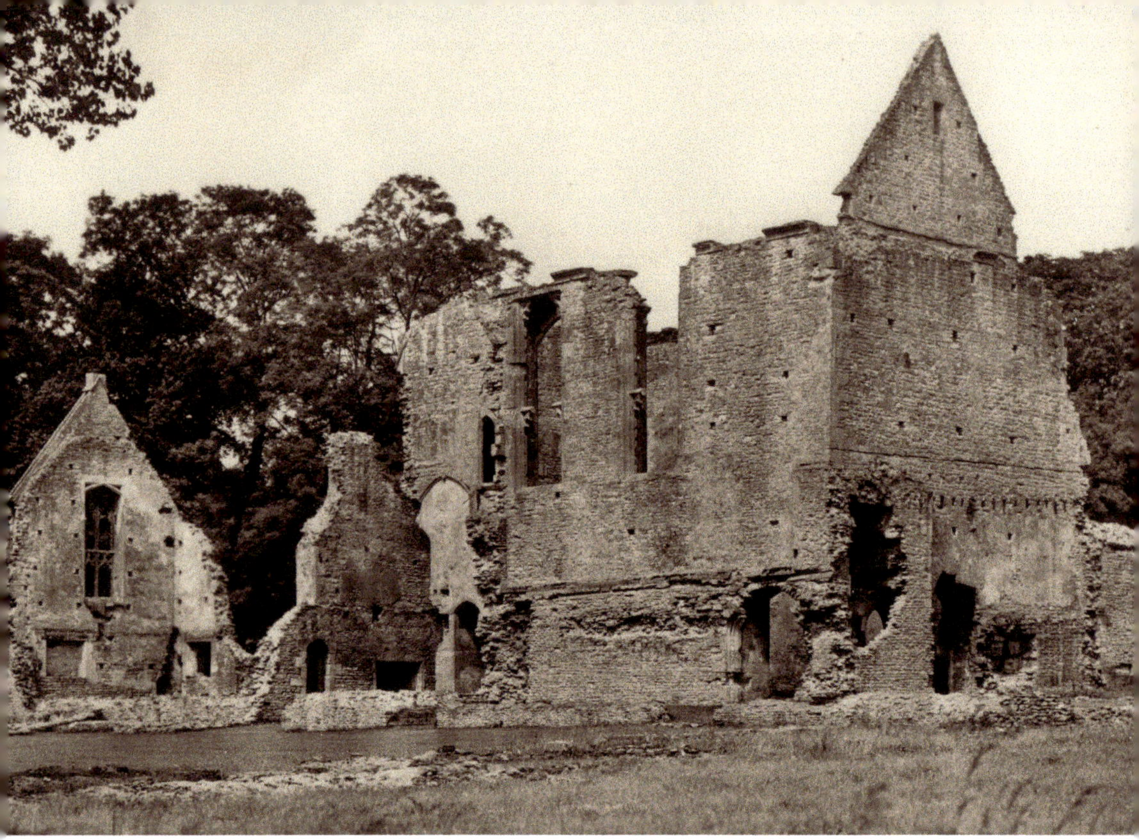

Above: The fifteenth-century manor house ruins, Minster Lovell.

Below: Ruins at Minster Lovell.

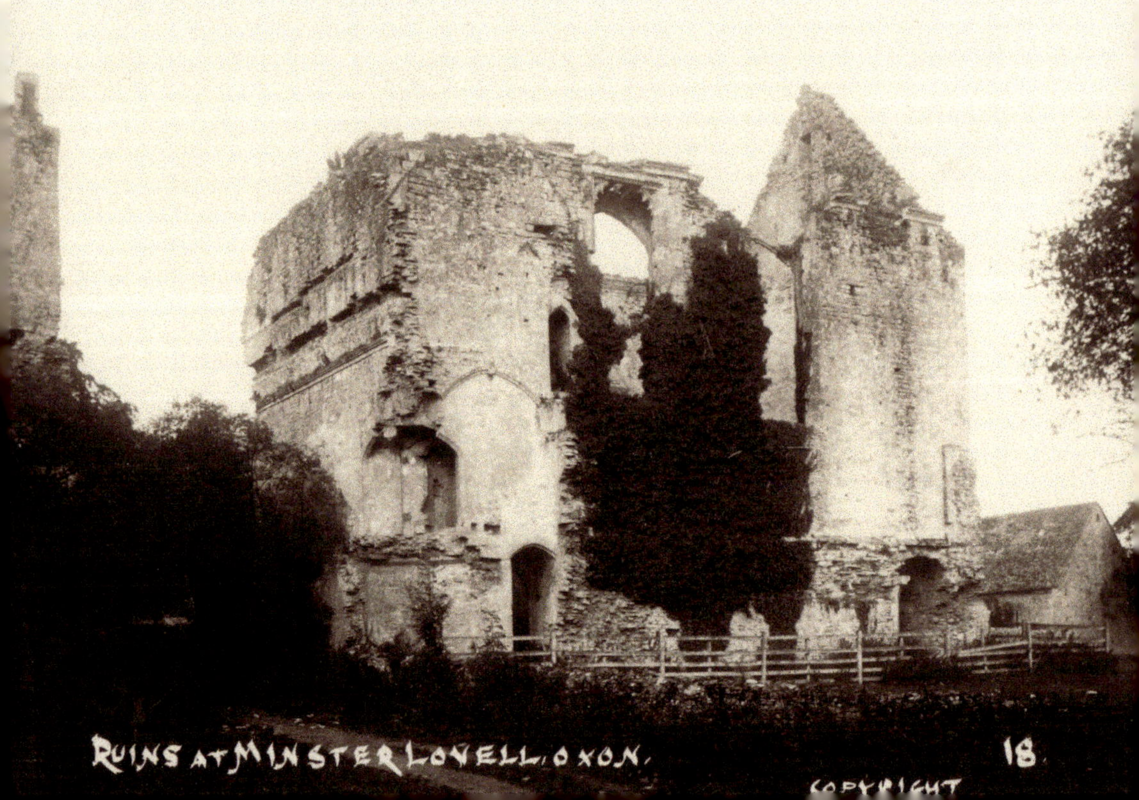

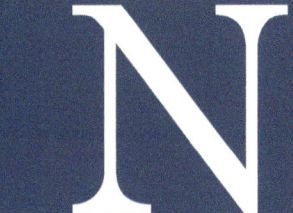

Nailsworth

This attractive little 'cloth' town, straddling the hillsides, is at the junction of two valleys and is bisected by the A46 Stroud Road. It has a twentieth-century clock tower marking its middle. It is made up of independent shops and at the centre, right on the A46, is William's Kitchen oyster bar and delicatessen, which has its own eatery. Everything looks very fresh and inviting. The old cloth mills on the main road are being reused, for example Egypt Mill is now a restaurant making a feature of the old mill workings displayed behind glass within the building. Ruskin Mill is an arts and crafts centre with its own café and there are 'Steiner influenced' lessons held here which make use of the lovely location down by the river and the woods up the hillside.

The clock tower in the centre of Nailsworth.

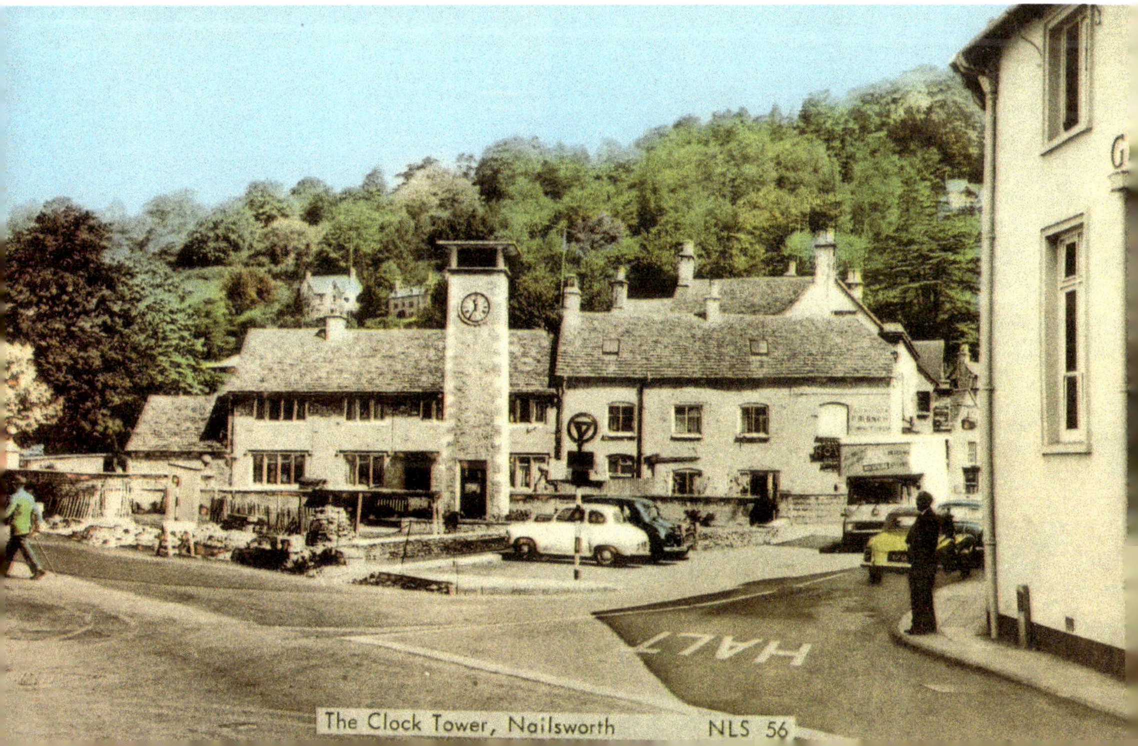

Nailsworth has its own literary connections. Along the road from Ruskin Mill is Horsley, which is home to the talented Kit Williams who wrote and illustrated *Masquerade* featuring local Nailsworth celebrities in the conundrum of a book which disguised clues as to where a golden treasure fashioned by Kit might be hidden. This caused a great deal of excitement as people tried to discover where the golden hare might be. Bamber Gascoigne was the only person besides Kit who knew the secret.

Going back into Nailsworth and exploring Watledge we come across a restored cottage on the hillside called Glendower. This was the final home of famous Welsh tramp-poet W. H. Davies who was much lauded in the 1930s. It is hoped that fans of his poetry will be able to access the cottage in the future for it has been restored in his honour and a collection of his poetry and his autobiography will be held there. It currently belongs to his great-nephew Norman Phillips and he hopes to keep it in the family where it belongs.

Northleach

Northleach is to be found 10 miles from Cirencester and was once on a coaching route between Oxford, Gloucester and north Wales until the bypass restored its peace and tranquillity. In the Middle Ages it was one of the most important wool-trading centres in the Cotswolds, rivalled only by Chipping Campden and Cirencester. Its magnificent wool church attests to its past. Its tower and south porch are amongst the finest in England. The clerestory windows illuminate the fine interior, including the contemporary goblet-shaped pulpit. The seating was designed by Sir Basil Spence and was made at Gordon Russell's furniture workshops in Broadway. Most interesting are the wool merchants' brasses often with symbols illustrating the trade, such as woolsacks, shears and sheep. Names like Thomas Bushe, who was merchant of the staple of Calais, John Taylour, William Midwinter, etc., are well known and enjoyed significant positions abroad as well as in this country.

To the east of the church is Northleach's square lined with shops, inns and houses dating from the sixteenth century to the early nineteenth century. In Northleach itself is a seventeenth-century almshouse, as well as Keith Harding's Mechanical Music Museum in the high street. Just to the east of the town is an eighteenth-century 'house of correction' or prison built by Sir George Onesiphorus Paul who was a philanthropist and reformer from a family of Huguenot clothiers from Woodchester who built Highgrove House. Talking of 'going off the rails', mention should be made of the TV award-winning comedy mockumentary *This Country* made in and around Northleach, written by and starring Daisy May Cooper as 'Kerry Mucklowe' and her brother Charlie Cooper as Kerry's cousin 'Kurtan', which should not be missed. Its theme is how difficult it is for the youth of this country to be raised in a rural setting.

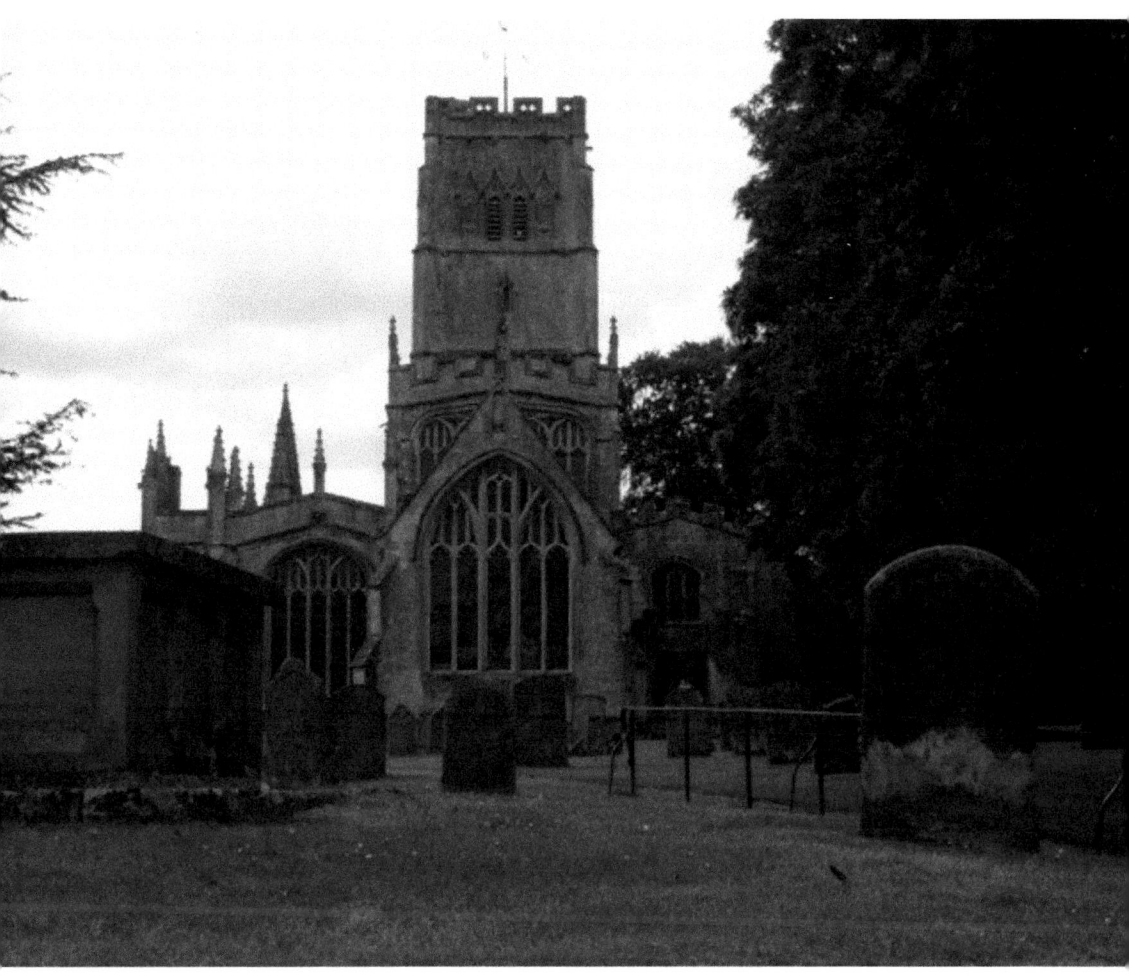

St Peter and St Paul's Church, Northleach – 'The Cathedral of the Cotswolds'.

Oddington

Oddington (Upper and Lower) lies 2.5 miles east of Stow-on-the-Wold and covers the lower slopes of the hill between Stow and the River Evenlode. Its remarkable buildings are the seventeenth-century Oddington House, also worked on in the nineteenth century, and the nearby rectory, with a similar story to tell. South of the village is the old church of St Nicholas, just off the Macmillan Way. As the church had seen some important owners including the Abbot of Gloucester, the Archbishop of York and various kings, such as Henry II, it is not surprising that work was carried out on the building in the thirteenth and fourteenth centuries but was untouched during the Victorian era, which has resulted in it being untampered with. (There is a nineteenth-century church in the main village.) Note in particular the Jacobean pulpit, the fifteenth-century font and the chancel roof. But most compelling of all is the large fourteenth-century Doom painting – on the north wall and possibly

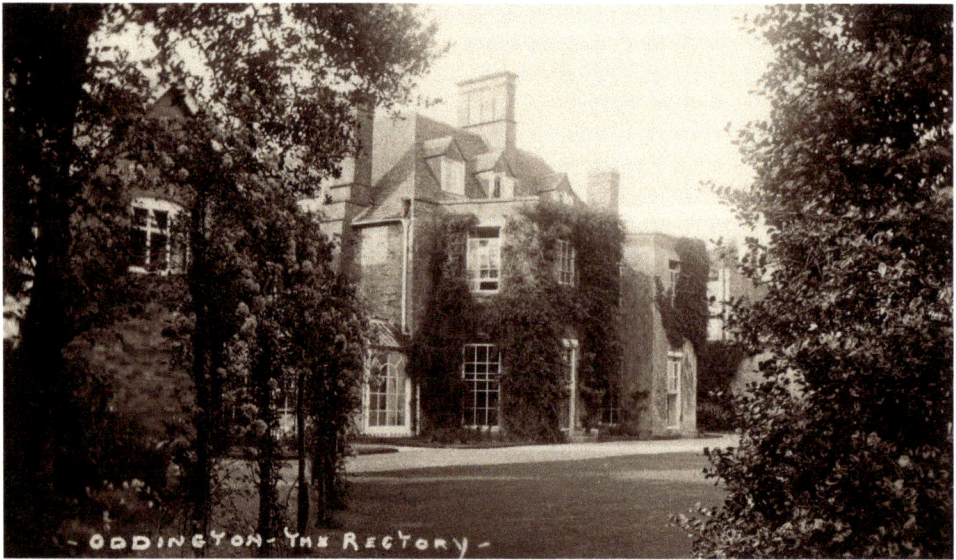

The rectory, Oddington.

the largest in the country – which certainly would have persuaded even the most recalcitrant parishioners to tow the line!

Owlpen

Owlpen is a cluster of buildings belonging to Sir Nicholas and Lady Mander, located in a wooded valley 3 miles east of the market town of Dursley and within walking distance of Uley. The main house is made up of three buildings built at different times which can be found below the compact Victorian Church of the Holy Cross. The main manor house is fifteenth century with sixteenth- and seventeenth-century additions and a small eighteenth-century mill nearby. Clipped yews frame the buildings.

The renowned architect Norman Jewson, a follower of Gimson and the Barnsley brothers, came across the Cotswold estate on one of his cycling tours from Sapperton after the poet Algernon Charles Swinburne had written to William Morris to tell him about it. He bought it, restored it in the 1920s but then ran out of capital. There are original seventeenth-century painted cloths – *Joseph and His Brothers* – in the Great Chamber or 'Queen Margaret's Room', as well as some glorious plaster animals like a hedgehog and owl on the walls in the Tudor Great Hall. There are also compatible Arts and Crafts furnishings throughout the house. In the medieval tithe barn there is a restaurant that sometimes served gravlax as Lady Mander is from Stockholm. The little church is lavishly decorated with gorgeous blue mosaics with plenty of gold – quite a delight to the eye. A mention should also be made

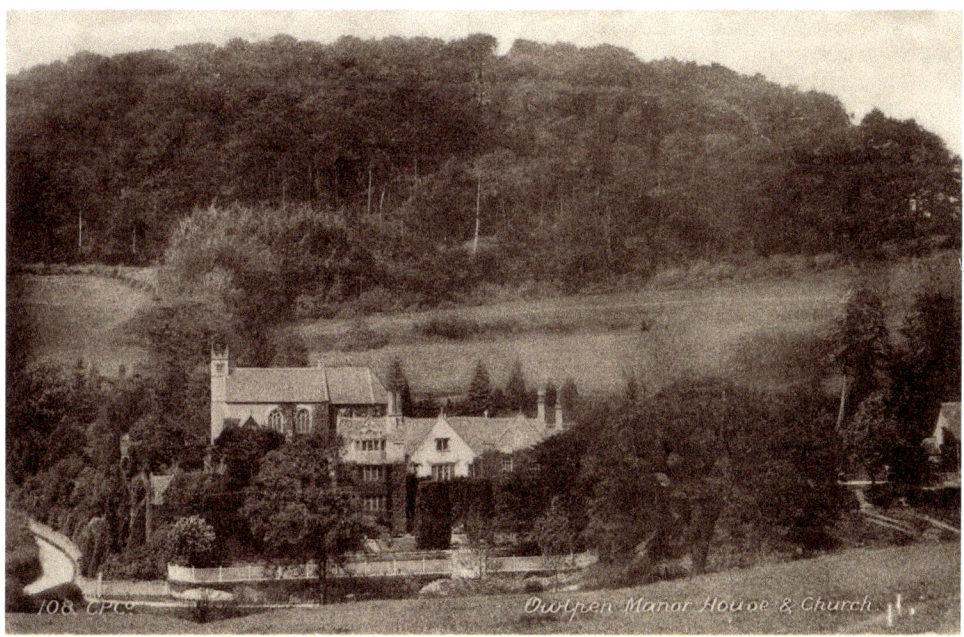

Owlpen Manor, near Uley.

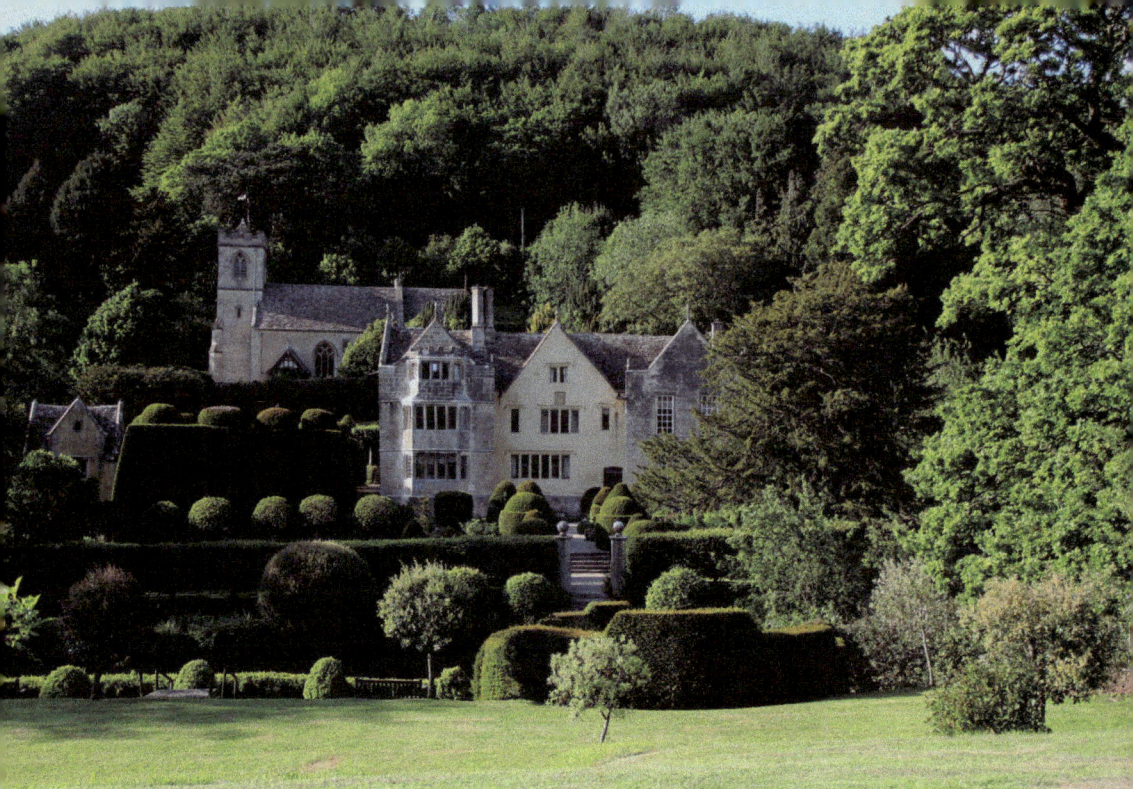

Owlpen.

of the outstanding terraced garden based on 'an early formal garden on a manorial scale'. There are seven hanging terraces created in the sixteenth and seventeenth centuries, so 'an historic survival' with yew topiary, old roses and box parterres. The paths and steps are quite uneven, so take care when walking on them.

Ozleworth

Ozleworth, called Oslan wyrth in 940, which might mean 'enclosure frequented by blackbirds' or that a man called Osla owned it, can be found down a winding lane 2.5 miles east of Wotton-under-Edge in a quiet wooded valley below Newark Park and a curious concrete telecommunications tower. There is a public footpath past the eighteenth-century Ozleworth Park and behind it is a compact Norman church to St Nicholas of Myra which stands in a circular churchyard, suggesting a more ancient use of the site, and boasts an unusual irregular hexagonal tower with a pyramidal roof. There is some impressive carving inside the church as well as a thirteenth-century font and four panels of sixteenth-century Flemish glass in the tower.

The church was decommissioned in the 1980s and is now in the care of the Churches Conservation Trust. Entry is round the back by the south doorway. The valley running southwards from here is Ozleworth Bottom, once home to several watermills used originally to grind corn in the sixteenth and seventeenth centuries and eventually converted to cloth mills, but long since demolished.

O

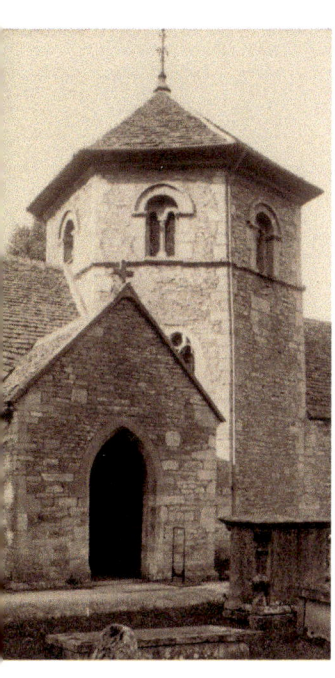 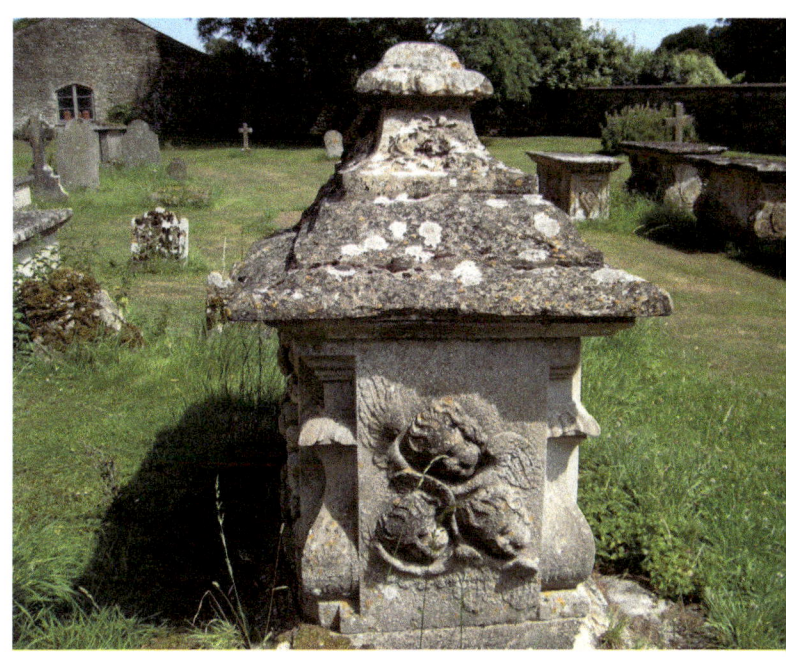

Above left and below: The twelfth-century Church of St Nicholas of Myra, Ozleworth.

Above right: Tomb in the circular churchyard.

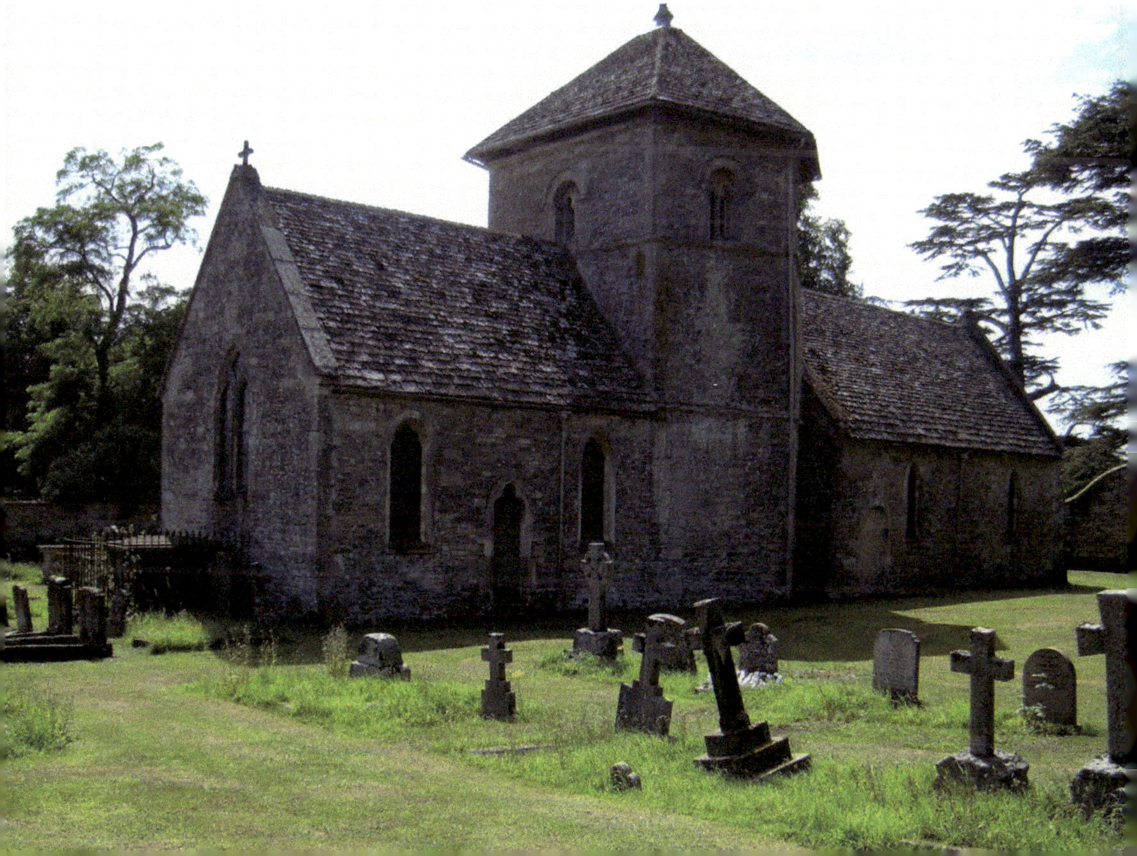

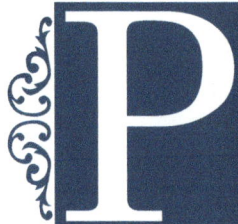

Painswick

Known as the 'Queen of the Cotswolds' because of its fine silver-grey limestone buildings, Painswick is 10 miles south-west of Cheltenham. There is an Iron Age defensive hill fort at Painswick Beacon, so the area was populated in early days. Painswick was just known as 'wicke' until 1237 when it became 'Painswik', deriving its name from 'Pain' taken from 'Pain' Fitzjohn, the lord of the manor, and 'wicke' meaning dairy farm. In the Middle Ages the village flourished because of the wool trade but between the sixteenth and eighteenth centuries cloth manufacture became the foremost occupation. South-facing attic rooms were the weavers' workshops and Flemish weavers settled here in the sixteenth century. By 1820 there were thirty mills on Painswick's fast-flowing pure streams. This prosperity can be traced in the buildings of the town: in fourteenth-century Bisley Street two houses have packhorse entrances which allowed the horses or donkeys laden with wool to pass.

The Falcon Hotel boasted the oldest bowling green in England, dating from 1554, while Painswick House had an early eighteenth-century 6-acre rococo garden which has been restored in recent years. Court House, dating from 1600, was a clothier's house and the intriguing Wool Drying Tower can be found in Kemp's Lane. Painswick Mill and King's Mill can still be seen to this day. Incidentally pin-making superseded the wool and cloth industries in Painswick.

Painswick's Grade I listed church of St Mary was originally built between 1042 and 1066 by Ernesi, an Anglo-Saxon thegn. It was extended in 1480 when the nave and tower were added, and its grand spire was added in 1632. There was damage during the Civil War when after the Siege of Gloucester the Royalists encamped overnight in Painswick, the King staying at Court House. There was some severe fighting and cannonballs damaged the tower of the church. In the churchyard there are fine table tombs dating from the seventeenth and eighteenth centuries, which was Painswick's most prosperous time as a cloth town. In 1792 ninety-nine yews were planted and it is said that the Devil takes the hundredth if anyone should try to plant one.

The 'clipping ceremony' is nothing to do with the yews, although they are neatly trimmed. It is held on the Sunday following the patronal festival and is from the Anglo-Saxon word 'clyppan', meaning to embrace. The children hold hands and encircle the church whilst singing a hymn, after which they are rewarded with a bun and a coin. Originally puppy dog pie was served, which was actually plum pudding with a china dog in it, first made in 1870. People from Painswick were once known as 'bow wows' and in fact in William Black's *Land That Thyme Forgot* he mentions a 'bow wow sauce' which was served with roast meats and developed in the town. In the eighteenth century a spurious 'tradition' was started by Benjamin Hyett based on a ceremony in antiquity when a procession dedicated to Pan took to the streets. While the deity was held aloft 'highgates, highgates' was chanted. This died out in the 1830s but was revived again in 1885 by the vicar, W. H. Seddon. It was finally laid to rest in the 1950s when Pan's statue was buried. It is thought that the statue may now somehow have made its way to the grounds of Painswick House.

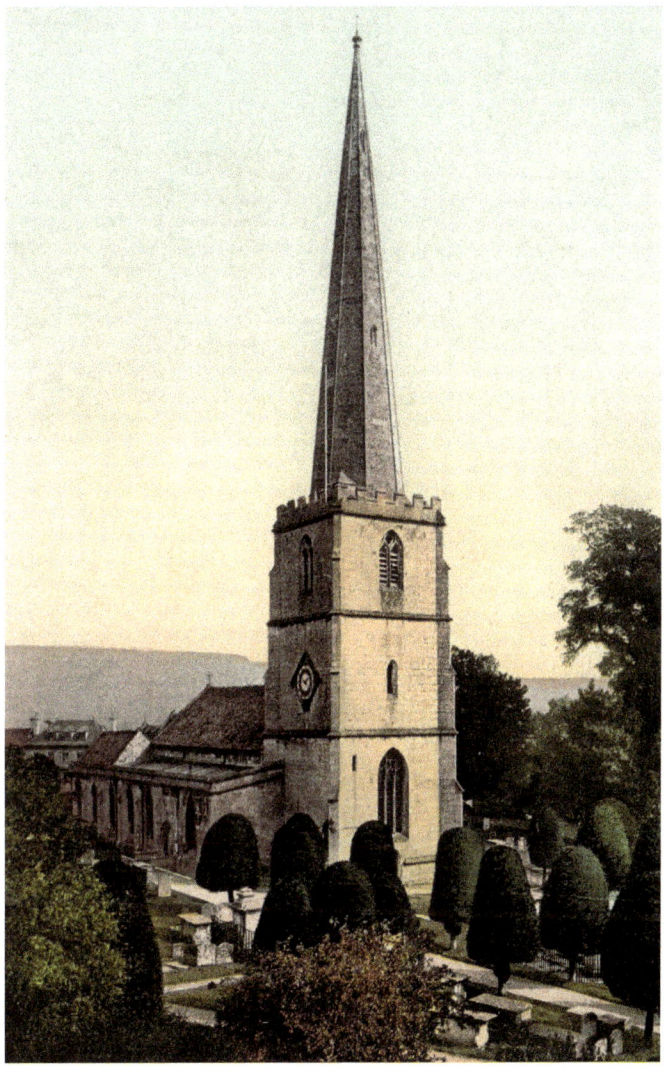

St Mary's Church, Painswick, surrounded by yews.

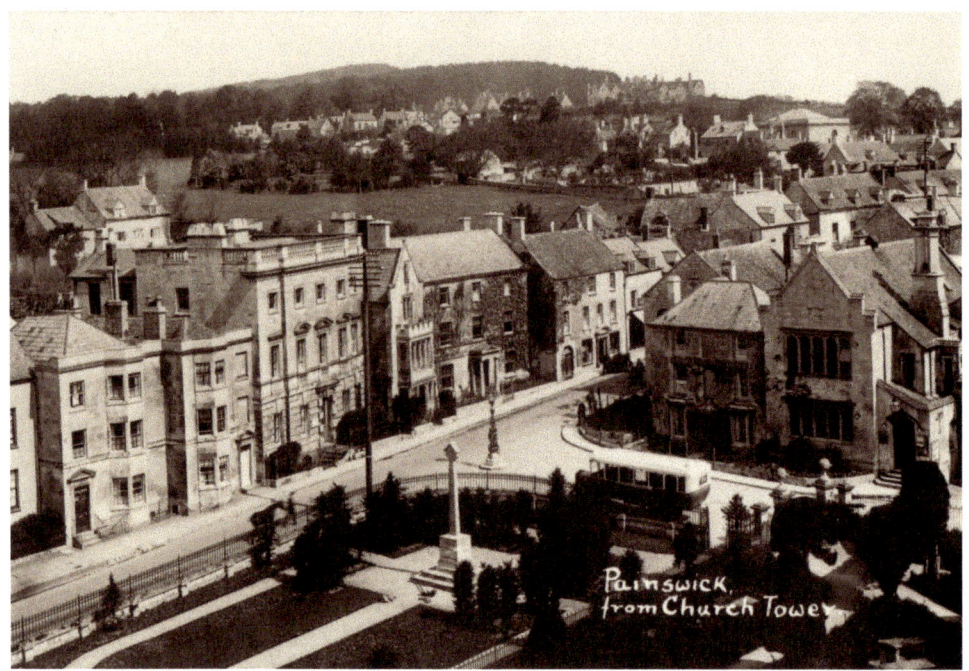

Above: Painswick from the church tower.

Below: Tibbiwell Street, Painswick.

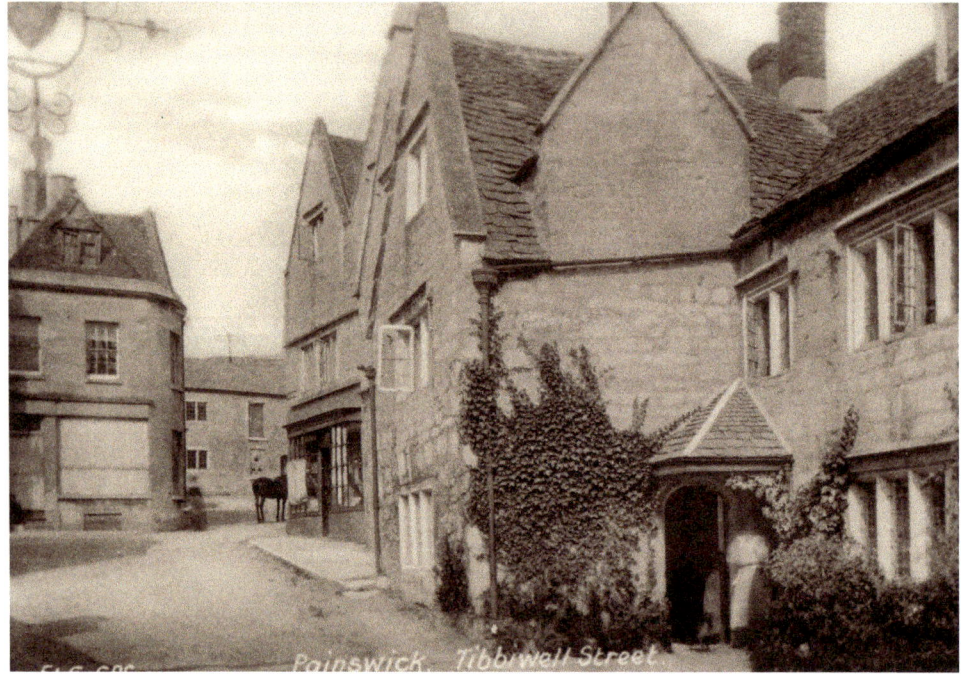

Prinknash Abbey

Prinknash Abbey is 2.5 miles north-east of Painswick. In 1928 a Benedictine community of six monks (others followed later) moved from Caldey Island off Pembrokeshire to this building. The 'old abbey' was built in the fourteenth century as a hunting lodge and grange for the Abbots of Gloucester. The 'new abbey' was constructed in 1972 using stone from Guiting quarries while the old building was re-roofed and refurbished and was opened as a retreat called St Peter's Grange. When the foundations of the new abbey were dug clay was found and so it was decided to try its most famous activity, pottery (with its recognisable 'pewter' glaze). The abbey also sells incense – it is the largest producer of incense in Europe – stained glass, vestments, and ironwork. Prinknash Bird Park is 9 acres of parkland with waterfowl, pygmy goats and fallow deer. After the dissolution the land was rented by Sir Antony Kingston who was to provide forty deer annually to Henry VIII, who used the house as a hunting lodge. As such, deer are a traditional part of the park.

In 2008 on 30 June (the feast of St Peter and St Paul) the community moved back into the old abbey building, selling the new one for luxury apartments.

In 1774 Horace Walpole wrote of Prinknash, 'It stands on a glorious but impracticable hill in the midst of a little forest of beech and commanding Elysium', and today the setting surveying the Vale of Gloucester is equally spectacular.

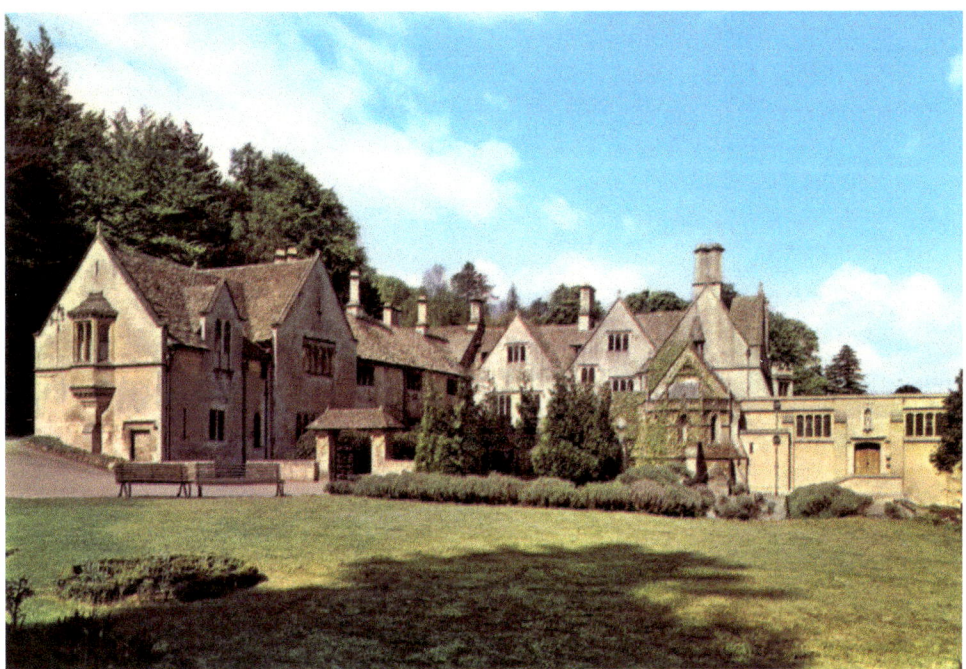

The old Benedictine abbey at Prinknash.

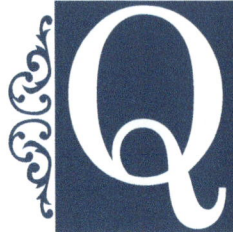

Quenington

Quenington is found 2 miles north of Fairford and very near Bibury, on the River Coln. Quenington Court is a largely nineteenth-century building, built on the 'site of a preceptory of the Knights Templar' which was later owned by the Knights Hospitaller. It has a fascinating thirteenth-century gatehouse and a round-shaped dovecote dating from the same period.

The Anglican church of St Swithin's, although much restored in the Victorian era, is a Grade I listed building originally built in the twelfth century. It was established in 1100 by the de Laci family and granted to St Peter's Abbey in Gloucester in 1138, but was taken over by the Knights Templar in 1193. The manor and living of the village was granted to the Hospitallers in 1312. Its twelfth-century Norman north and south doorways should not be missed. Over the north doorway is the Harrowing of Hell, which is always intriguing, but the tympanum over the south doorway is the oldest known Coronation of the Virgin in Europe still in situ. Both are outstanding examples of Romanesque carving.

Quenington boasts an award-winning pub, the Keepers Arms, for those in need of refreshment.

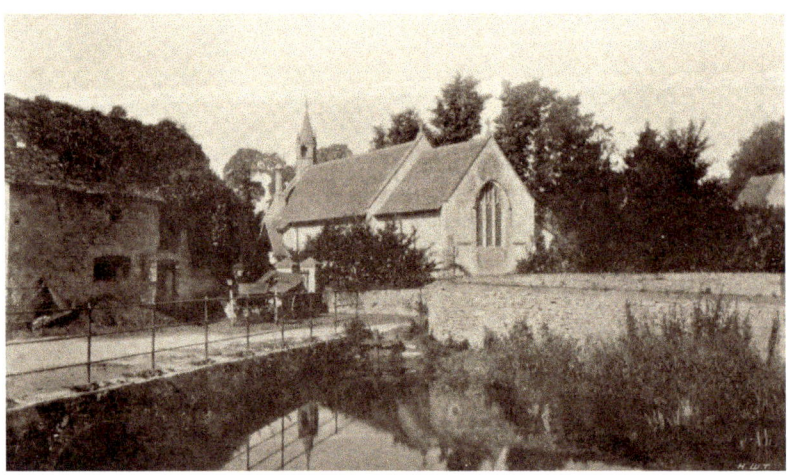

St Swithin's Church, Quenington, from the Coln.

Quinton, Upper and Lower

These were two of seven manors granted to Hugh de Grandmesnil after the Norman Conquest and are 6 miles south of Stratford-upon-Avon. Now they are in Warwickshire but were originally in Gloucestershire. This is how they were described at the time:

> The same Hugh holds Upper Quinton. There are two hides. The thegn held it. Its desmesne two ploughs and five villans and one bordars with three ploughs. There are four slaves and one female slave. It was worth £7 now £4.
>
> The same Hugh holds Lower Quinton and Roger holds of him. There are twelve hides. Baldwin held it TRE. Its desmesne three ploughs and seventeen villans and two bordars with nine ploughs.
>
> There are six slaves. It was worth £7 now £6.

Most of Lower Quinton is still unspoilt. It has a number of thatched timber-framed cottages around a village green, with a seventeenth-century yellow-brick house with Cotswold tiles and an attractive pub, the College Arms. This shows the arms of Magdalene College, Oxford, which owns much of the land in the area. Lower Quinton church is nearby with its 130-foot spire. The church dates back to Norman days, with its south arcading and font from that time. There is a Perpendicular clerestory and look out for the effigy of Sir William Clopton, who fought at Agincourt and whose wife took a vow of widowhood at his death, becoming an 'anchorite' (a type of hermit), in a cell close by. Across the fields at Upper Quinton there is a timber-framed manor house and to the south is Meon Hill belonging to Lower Quinton – a northern outpost of the Cotswolds – and the site of the witchcraft-related murder in 1945 of Charles Walton.

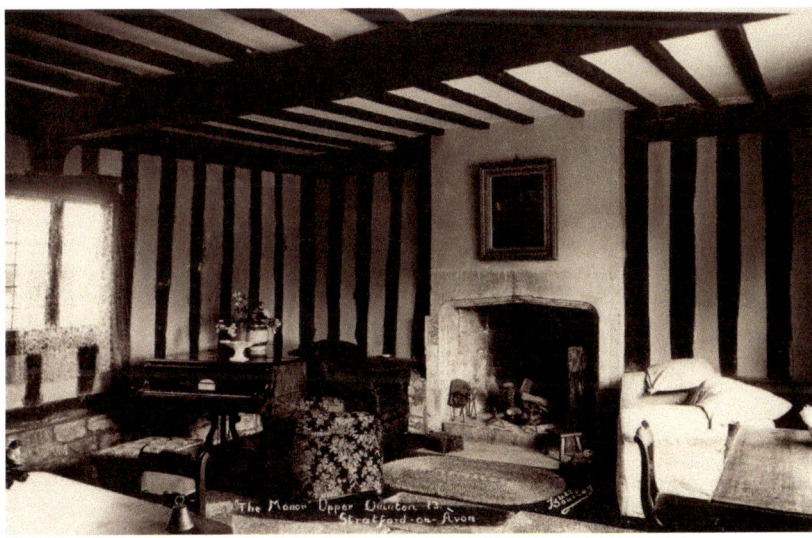

The old Manor, Upper Quinton.

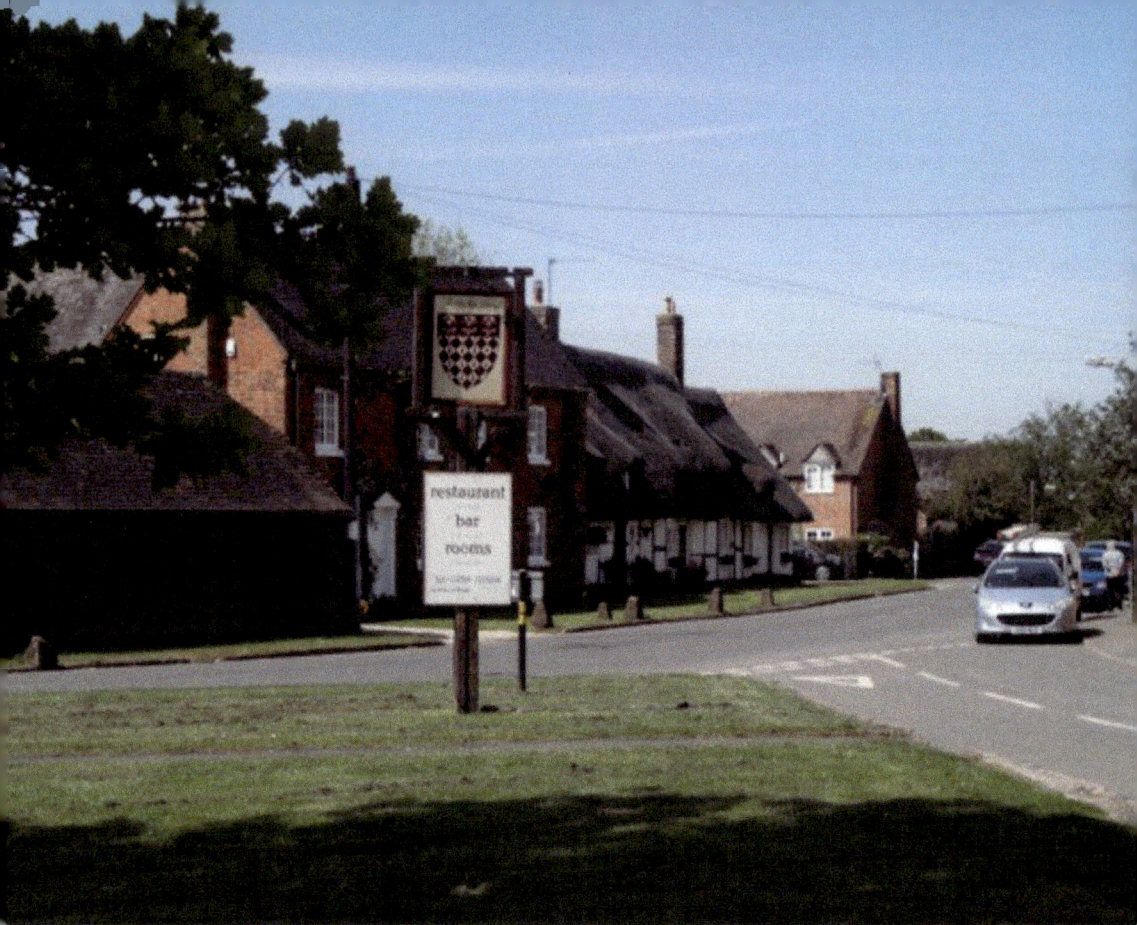

The College Arms, Lower Quinton.

R

Randwick

Although some of Randwick is a suburb of Stroud, a great deal of it still retains its village character. It is situated on the slopes below Standish Woods (where there are two round barrows and a long barrow) around a mile and a half north-west of Stroud. There is a Victorian church with a Perpendicular tower surrounded by a shady churchyard. This is the focus of the ancient Randwick 'Wap' dating back to the Middle Ages, held on the first Sunday in May. Three cheeses arrive on litters bedecked with flowers, they are blessed and then rolled three times round the church, after which

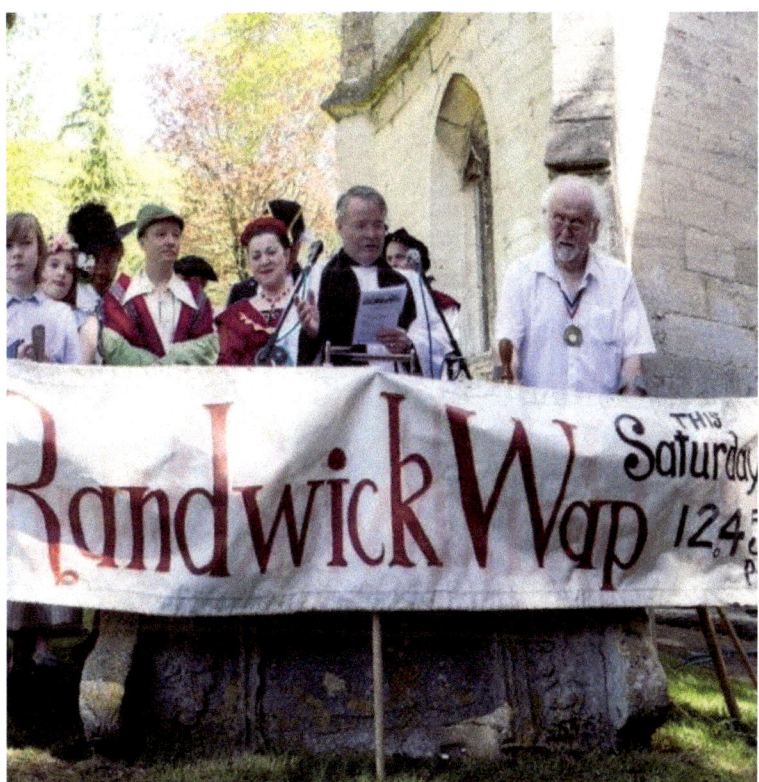

The Randwick Wap celebrations.

they are cut up by personages in ceremonial uniform. On the following Sunday there is a mock-mayor-making ceremony. After the festivities be sure to find the nearby Vine Tree Inn for refreshment.

Rodborough

This village, a mile south-west of Stroud, has now become a hilly suburb. In 1900 its manor was consumed by fire – it had once been the home of the Huguenot prison reformer Sir George Onesiphorus Paul.

Up on Rodborough Common, buffeted by the wind, is Rodborough Fort, built in 1761 as a 'pleasure house' for local dyer George Hawker with a typically Victorian frontage (it was rebuilt in 1870). Most of the common land here was given to the National Trust in 1937 by Thomas Bainbrigge Fletcher, an entomologist. There are superb views from here of the valleys below, and do not miss the Bear of Rodborough for refreshment.

Incidentally Rodborough was the home of Benjamin Bucknell, who designed Woodchester Mansion, and the Revd Awdry, who wrote *Thomas the Tank Engine* and the other railway books. Awdry lived in Rodborough Avenue for thirty years until his death in 1997.

Rodborough Fort.

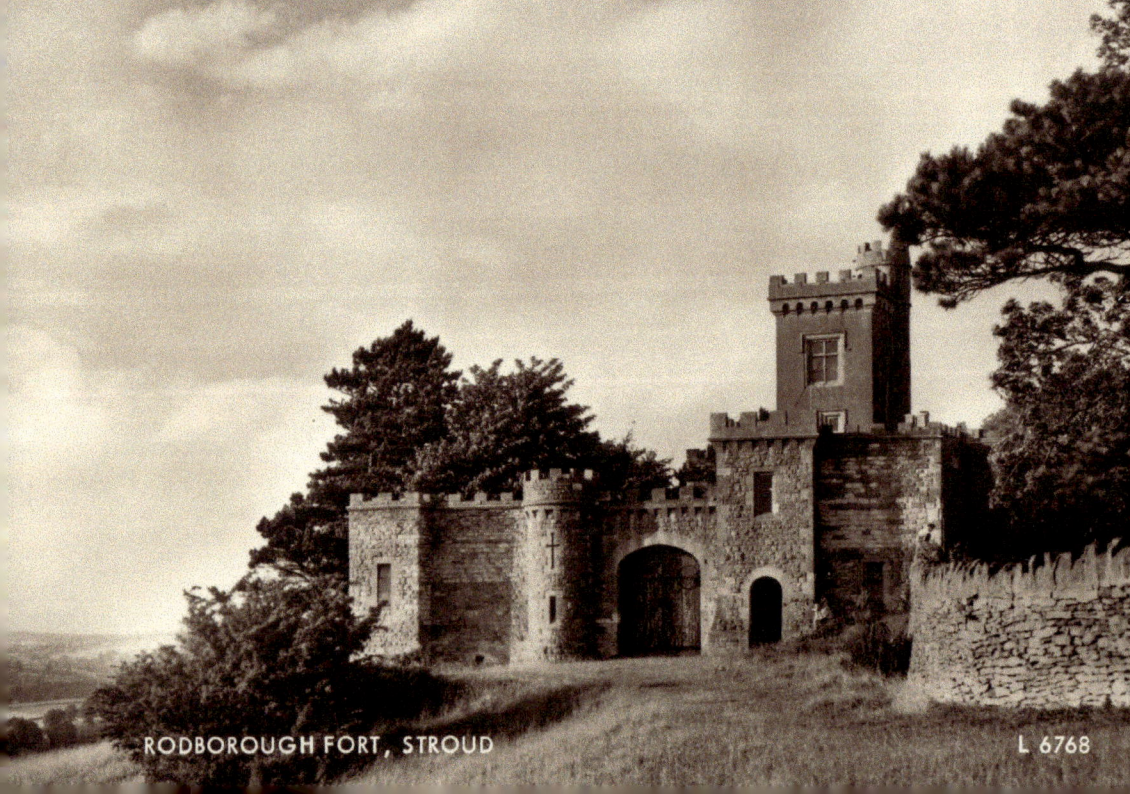

Rodmarton

There are cottages around a small green, with a spired church nearby with pollarded trees round the gate in Rodmarton village, which is found 4.5 miles north-east of Tetbury. Inside the church, although over-restored by the Victorians, there are some good stone floors, a brass dating to the fifteenth century of a lawyer in his professional garb and eighteenth- and nineteenth-century monuments. Of particular interest is the manor house found nearby, built between 1909 and 1926 to the designs of Ernest Barnsley. Claud Biddulph had instructed Ernest Barnsley to build a new Arts and Crafts building from scratch, which was to be known as Rodmarton Manor. The house was built of local materials, locally sourced timber and stone, using estate workers and local specialist craftsmen but using no machinery and to techniques which pre-dated the Industrial Revolution. It was furnished with items by Ernest, his brother Sidney, Ernest Gimson and Peter Waals. Some furniture was bought which was made by craftsmen Harry David, Owen Scrubey and Oliver Mord. Pottery was painted by Alfred and Louise Powell. Wall hangings were made by Hilda Benjamin

The iconic Arts and Crafts building, Rodmarton Manor.

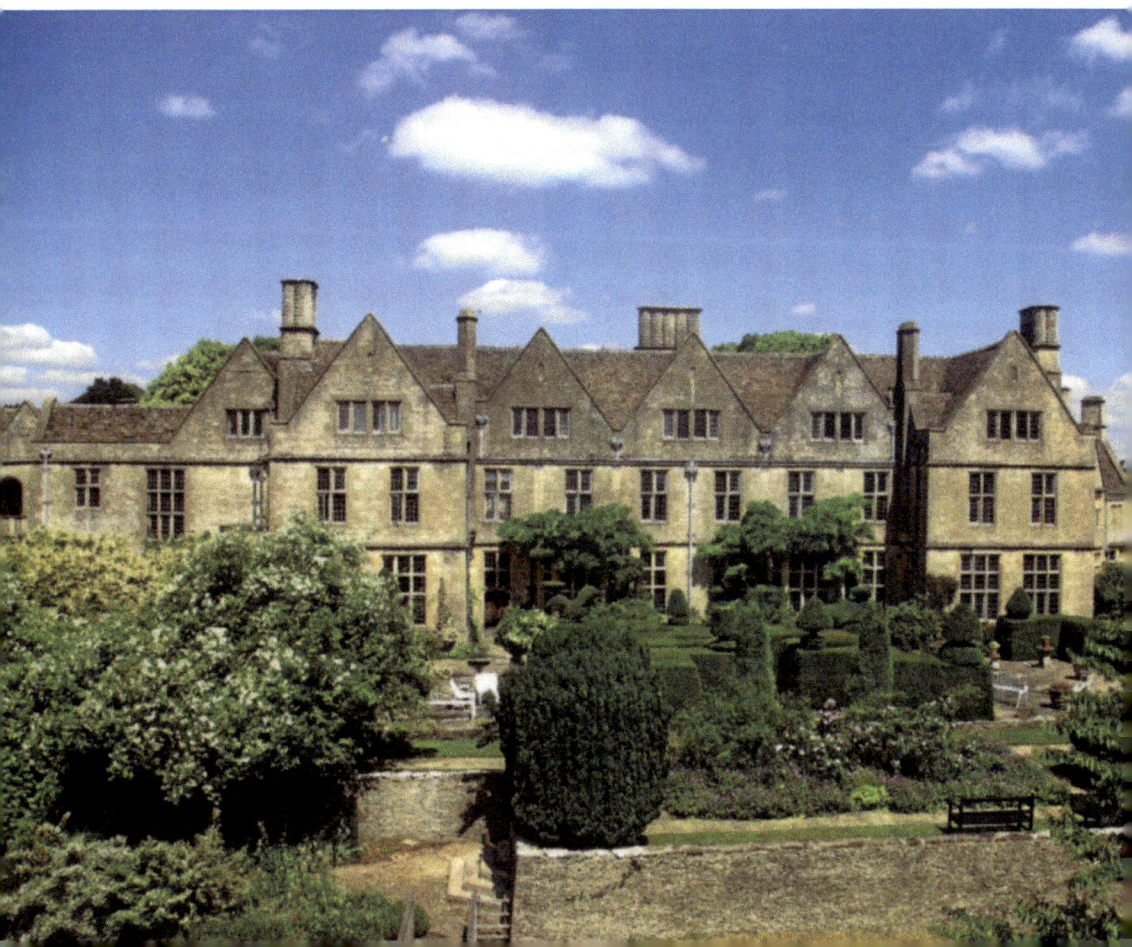

while brass and leadwork was carried out by Norman Jewson, who renovated Owlpen Manor. Ironwork was by Fred and Frank Baldwin and Alfred Bucknell. The Biddulphs moved into the east wing but the rest was given over to community activities such as musical evenings, poetry recitals, puppet shows and craft classes. The celebrated Cotswold garden is spectacular in the summer and shouldn't be missed.

Rollright Stones

The fascinating ancient Rollright Stones can be found 2.5 miles north-west of Chipping Norton (rollright meaning a wheel enclosure, or possibly from the Old English Hrollalandriht, meaning land held by a Saxon named Hrolla). They are made of local oolitic limestone and are possibly associated with ancestor veneration on sacred ground – at the time when our predecessors were beginning to settle and farm. The stones include the King's Men, a late Neolithic to early Bronze Age circle of weathered standing stones dating to around 1900 BC, and measuring around 100 feet in diameter. Some 400 yards to the east is the burial chamber or dolmen known as the Whispering Knights because of its rather sinister appearance and dating to the Early or Middle Neolithic era. These are in Oxfordshire while across the road in Warwickshire is the King's Stone, an isolated standing stone and possible Bronze Age grave marker, somehow associated with the stone circle. Every year a festival of celebration by the contemporary pagans is held here and there is a ceremony celebrating the winter solstice. There are fine views from this upland country at any time of year.

This is part of the Jurassic Way, which stretches along the limestone ridge from the Humber to Salisbury Plain and beyond. There is a legend that a king, intent on conquering Britain, was told by a witch 'If Long Compton thou dost see, King of England thou shalt be.' This turned out to be impossible, so the king, his men and knights were transformed to stone and the witch to an elder tree.

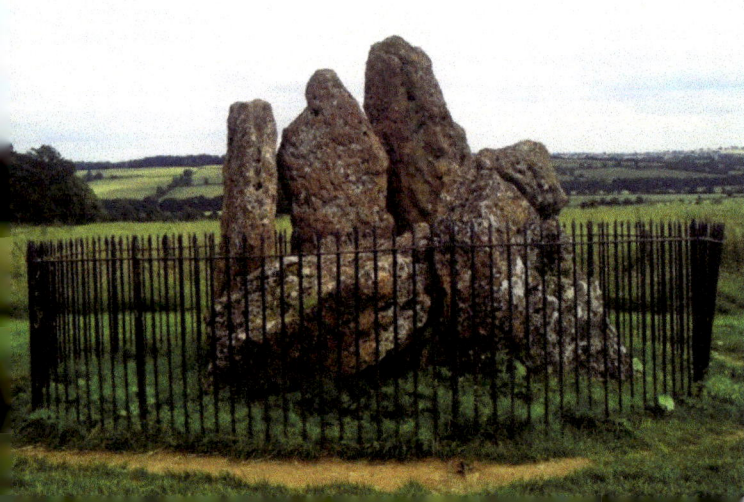

The Whispering Knights dolmen dates to around 3800 BC.

S

Sapperton

Sapperton (listed as Sapleton in the Domesday Book) is a truly picturesque village found 5 miles west of Cirencester and which is adjacent to the western end of Cirencester Park, above the Frome Valley. It is famous for the Sapperton Canal (legging) Tunnel, which is 3,817 yards long, emerging north-west at Daneway, and it was visited by George III during its construction in 1788.

The church of St Kenelm's was rebuilt during the reign of Queen Anne and is mostly eighteenth century with round-headed windows in the original glass. Beneath its yew trees near the entrance to the churchyard are the graves of the great Arts and Crafts craftsmen Ernest Gimson (1864–1919), Ernest Barnsley (1863–1926) and his brother Sidney Barnsley (1865–1926). When they first arrived in the area they were given the opportunity by Lord Bathurst to live in Pinbury Park on a repairing lease, before the

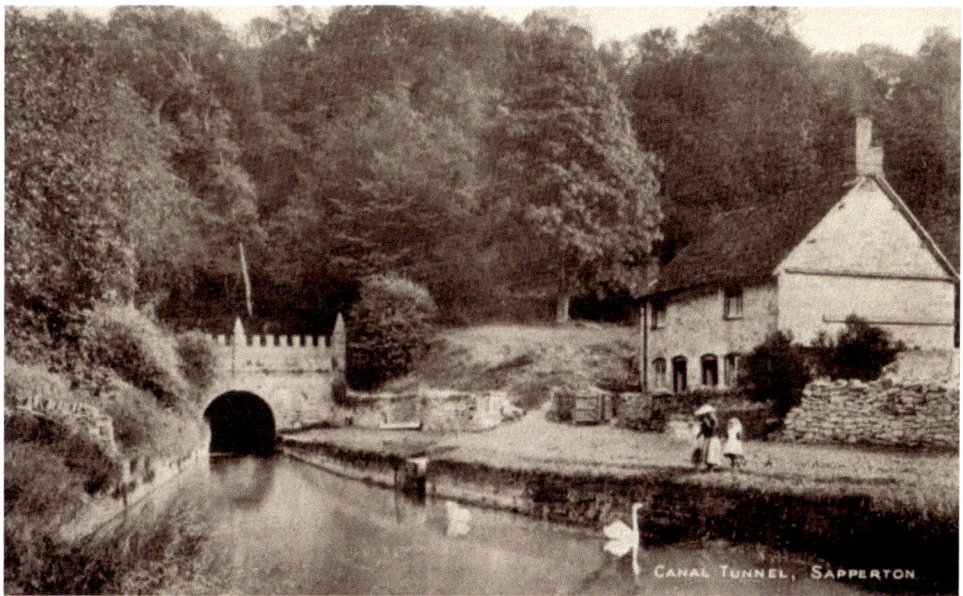

Sapperton Canal tunnel.

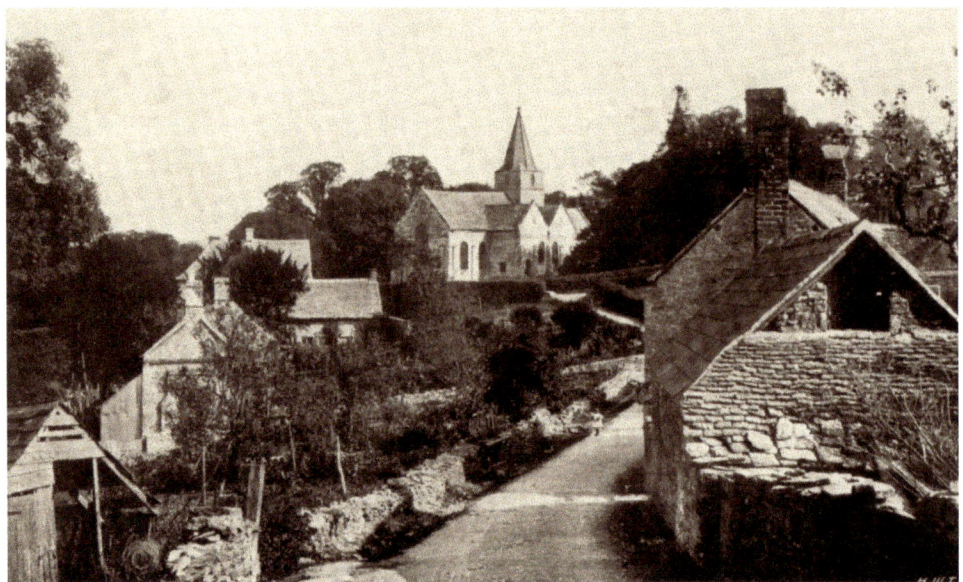

Where Gimson and the Barnsley brothers built their homes.

Bathursts took it over as their own. In fact Lord Bathurst was so pleased with their work that he offered the craftsmen land in the village to build their own cottages: north-east of the church can be found Upper Dorvel House and Beechowes, built by Sidney and Ernest Barnsley; and Leasehowes, by Ernest Gimson. Ernest Barnsley's son-in-law Norman Jewson lived at Bachelor's Court.

Ernest Barnsley was commissioned by Countess Bathurst to design a building for use by the community in 1912 in the former wheelwrights yard, and the Grade II listed Sapperton Village Hall was presented to the village in 1969 by Lord Bathurst. A multi-award-winning pub, the Bell, is in the village. It welcomes dogs and has horse parking outside!

Sezincote

Sezincote, near Moreton-in-Marsh, once a small medieval village, was bought in 1765 by Colonel John Cockerell who had returned from Bengal. He left the estate to his younger brother, Charles, who had also worked for the East India Company and in turn he employed his brother Samuel Pepys Cockerell, surveyor to the East India Company, as his architect to work with Thomas Daniel, an artist recently returned from India. Together they came up with an impressive house plan in the Indian style. Inspiration came from the sixteenth-century Mughal Emperor Akbar who had taken Hindu and Islamic influences, combining the two cultures. Something unique happened in the English setting when a fine red-sandstone house with copper dome

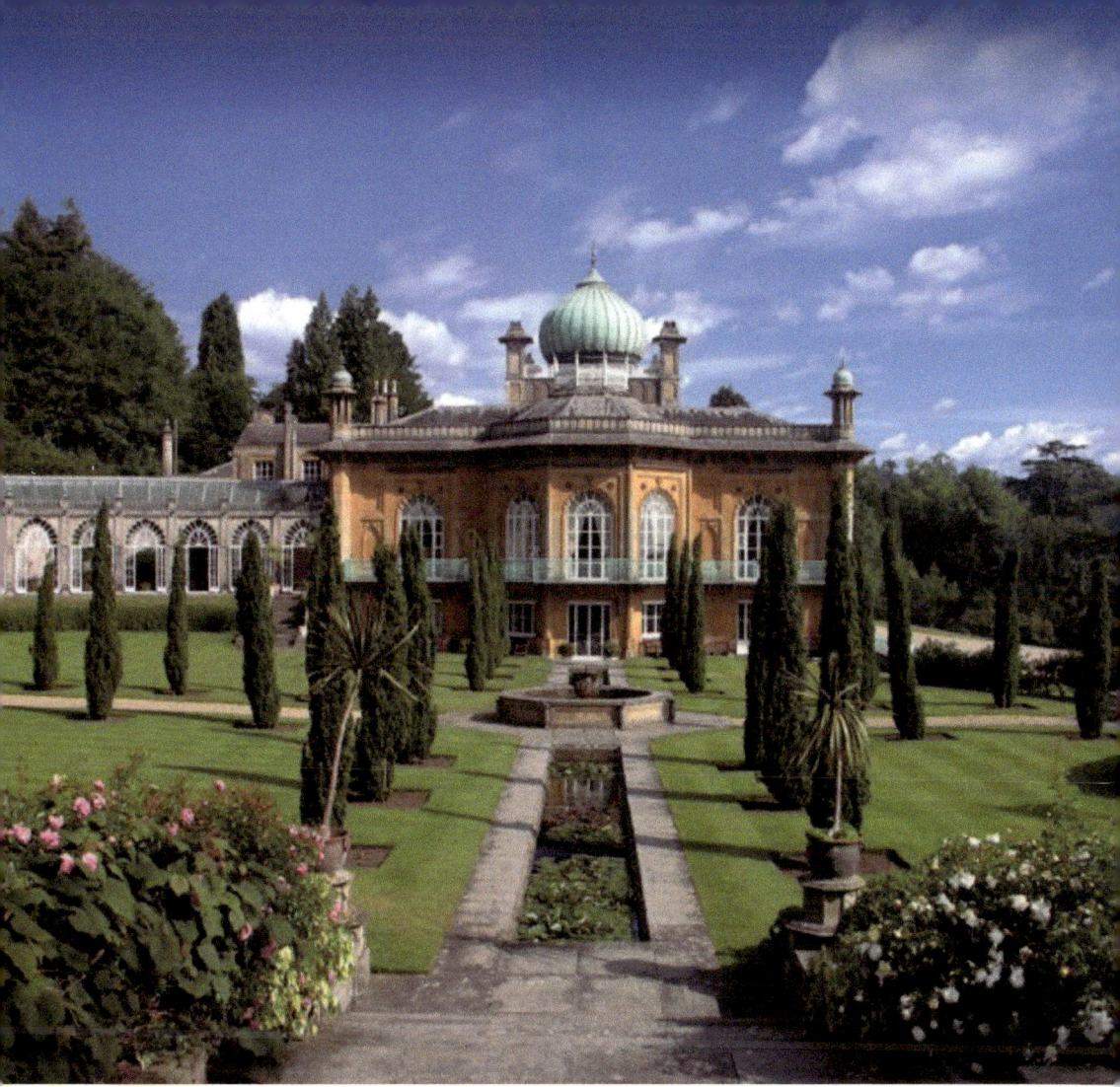

Sezincote is around 200 years old.

appeared in 1805 in the Mughal style, enhanced by water gardens and lakes created by Humphry Repton. There are elements of Hindu style in the crescent bridges with columns.

Read John Betjeman's *Summoned by Bells* for a flavour of the house parties held in the classic interior of Sezincote in the 1930s. The Prince Regent had visited in 1806 and he was so impressed by Sezincote that he commissioned his architect, John Nash, to do something similar with his Pavilion at Brighton.

Slimbridge

Travel down to Slimbridge on the A38, 12 miles from Gloucester, and the character changes almost as soon as you enter the village. It is a rustic ride past red-brick buildings, the thirteenth-century church in the Early English style, the farmyard entrances and down past the Tudor Arms, across the canal bridge and on till you reach the relatively modern building of the Wildfowl and Wetlands Trust. This organisation, project of Sir Peter Scott and created in 1946, was originally called the Severn Wildfowl Trust, then simply the Wildfowl Trust, but changed its name to the fuller title in the 1980s or 1990s when it was realised that habitats were paramount for the survival of the birds.

The organisation has four aims: education, research, conservation and recreation. Indeed as the years have passed emphasis has changed to it being a tourist attraction as finance has been needed to support the organisation in its other aims. Peter Scott had originally chosen this spot as he had visited it as a wildfowler then birder looking for white-fronted and lesser white-fronted geese on their feeding grounds of the Dumbles, on the edge of the estuary. He decided to build a reserve here where he could feed wild birds as well as keeping his collection of tame waterfowl from all over the world. A series of ponds were built, fed by a circular system of water from the Severn. A fox-proof fence was built around the outside of the reserve to keep the captives safe.

The land had belonged to the Berkeley Estate and conveniently an old piped duck decoy, once used for catching ducks for food, was enclosed within the reserve which

The Slimbridge Wildfowl and Wetlands Trust started by Sir Peter Scott.

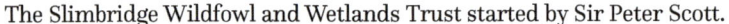

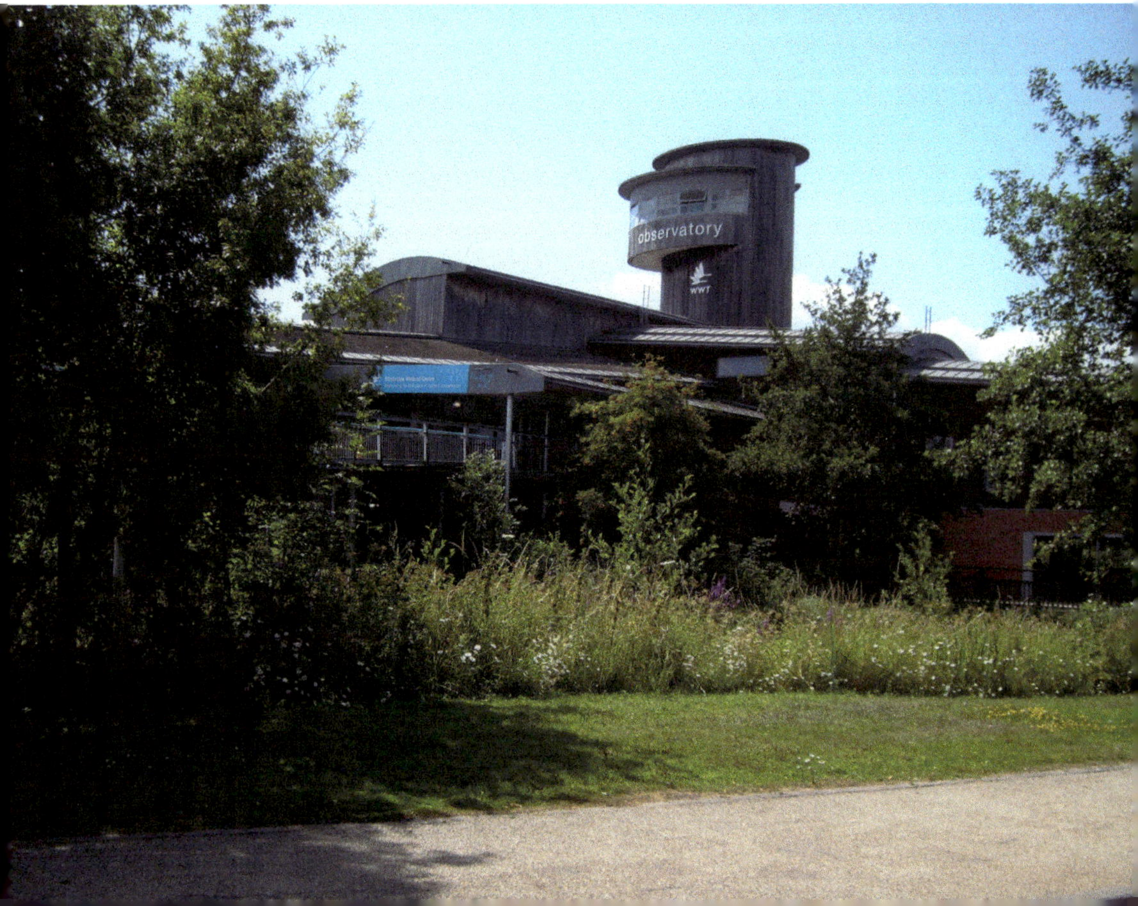

could be used for capturing birds for ringing, measuring and weighing to keep scientific records. In another part of the grounds outside the reserve a hatchery was built for captive breeding birds which were endangered, and within the grounds a tropical house was built, as well as houses for birds like the six species of flamingos which needed protection from the elements.

To begin with there were gentlemen in plus-fours who were birders staffing the grounds, but as time went on things changed. A restaurant and shop was built, and there was a 100-seat lecture theatre that was decorated to look like the bottom of a pond. The Trust has now established other reserves, at Peakirk, Cambridgeshire; Martin Mere, Lancashire; Washington, Tyne and Wear; Arundel, Sussex; Llanelli, South Wales; Caerlaverock, Scotland; and, most recently, Barnes in London.

Peter Scott's home at Slimbridge is to open as a museum to honour the great man, and people will be able to see where he lived and worked, producing the paintings he continued to do all his life.

When visiting make sure to see the birds Peter Scott and the team have been responsible for saving, such as the docile nenes that feed out of your hand, the cranes that have been reintroduced into the Somerset Levels, the wild birds you can watch feeding out towards the Severn Estuary and, as it gets dark in winter, the murmurations of starlings wheeling around the open skies above Slimbridge.

Stow-on-the-Wold

'Stow-on-the-Wold, where the wind blows cold', as the old saying goes, is in an elevated position at 800 feet above sea level and at the junction of the major roads running through the Cotswolds.

There was an Iron Age settlement here and a Roman villa nearby, but the town was founded by the Normans, who wanted to take advantage of the passing trade. Stow was originally known as Stow St Edward or Edwardstow after the town's patron saint, which may be Edward the Martyr or possibly Edward the Confessor. While a small settlement, it was controlled by the abbot of the local abbey and when the first market was held here, granted by Henry I, the proceeds went to Evesham Abbey.

In 1330 Edward III granted an annual seven-day fair to be held here in August. In 1476 Edward IV made this two five-day fairs in May around the feast days of St Philip and St James and another in October to mark the feast of Edward the Confessor. These 'charter fairs' took place in the market square. They were renowned for the sale of wool and sheep. Daniel Defoe observed that in the early eighteenth century as many as 20,000 sheep were sold in one day. Alleyways known as 'lures' were used to herd the sheep into the square. The town began to grow prosperous and handmade goods began to be sold. As the wool trade declined the horse trade developed, and this still takes place in a field near Maugersbury every May and October. This used to bring trade into the town but now inns and shops tend to close for fear of theft or vandalism.

The last battle of the Civil War took place a mile north of Stow on 21 March 1646. At first it seemed that the Royalists had the upper hand but the Parliamentarians routed the Royalists, who fought a running battle back into Stow where they surrendered in the market square. This has become known as the Battle of Stow.

Of interesting people and events connected with Stow, John Entwistle of The Who lived here for thirty years. Henry Ferguson, inventor of the famous tractor, died here. An edition of *Top Gear* was filmed here, but more appropriately Adam Henson, dressed in an English tweed suit, drove his sheep through the streets of Stow in a demonstration of how good English wool is, as a protest against the poor price fleece fetches these days. This was shown on *Countryfile*.

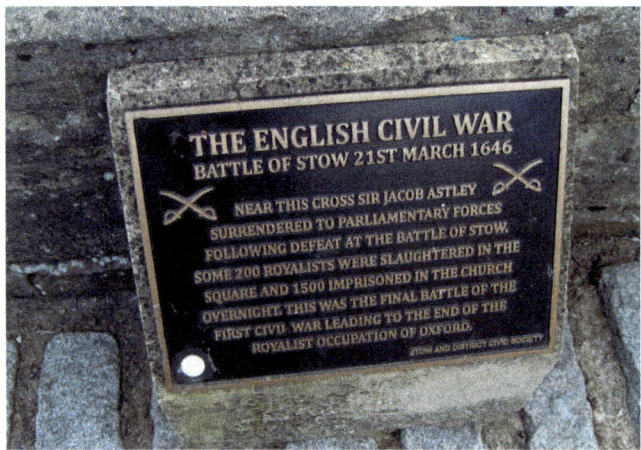

Left: Stow war memorial.

Below: Market Place at Stow.

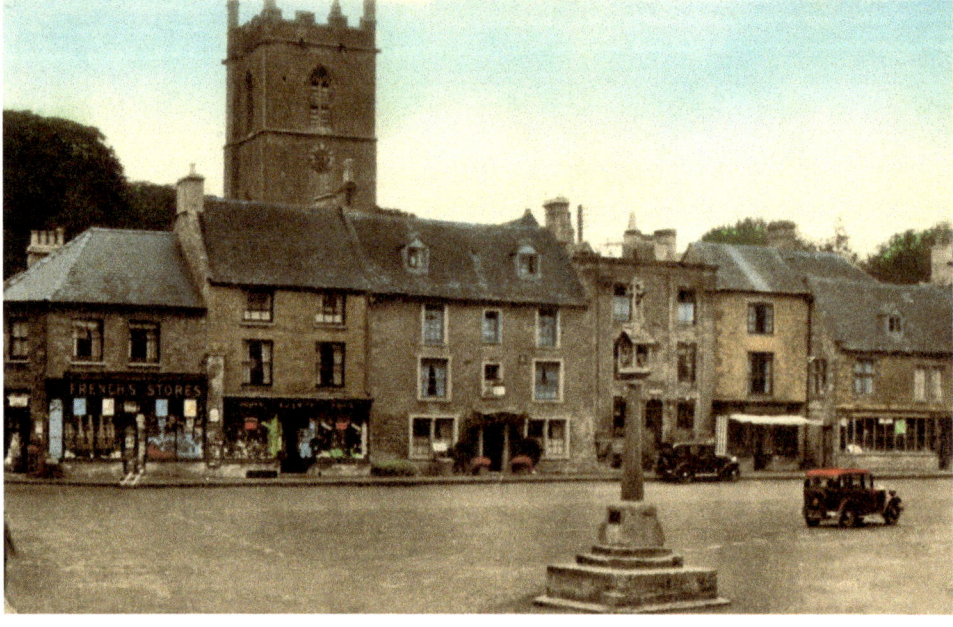

Stroud

At 8 miles from Gloucester, Stroud is a bustling market town with a lively café culture, being the first town in the country to have a truly organic café in Woodruffs, and it has an award-winning farmers' market started in 1999 by Jasper Conran and Isabella Blow. At one time there was a South American-themed shop in one of its streets and Stroud residents gloried in the colourful chunkily knitted jumpers – but alas this has long since closed down.

It is a culturally diverse and artistic community with many writers, artists, actors and musicians taking up residence in the area. Damien Hirst has not one, but two studios locally. Stroud promotes renewable energy, saving trees from unnecessary destruction, and there is a Stroud pound to help the local economy. It has been described as 'Notting Hill with wellies'! The town itself has steep streets of independent shops and its appearance might belie the vibrant culture which Stroud boasts. It was known as 'La Strode' in the thirteenth century and, lying at the meeting point of five valleys, there was abundant water for woollen mills while the sheep grazed on the hills above, and there were minerals available for the dyeing process. Indeed Stroud was renowned for its scarlet cloth called 'Stroudwater scarlet', which furnished military uniforms. At one time there were 150 mills in the valleys around Stroud.

In the seventeenth century there was a Huguenot community which had fled persecution in France and in the nineteenth century a Jewish contingent associated with tailoring and the cloth industry. Although that textile activity has long since

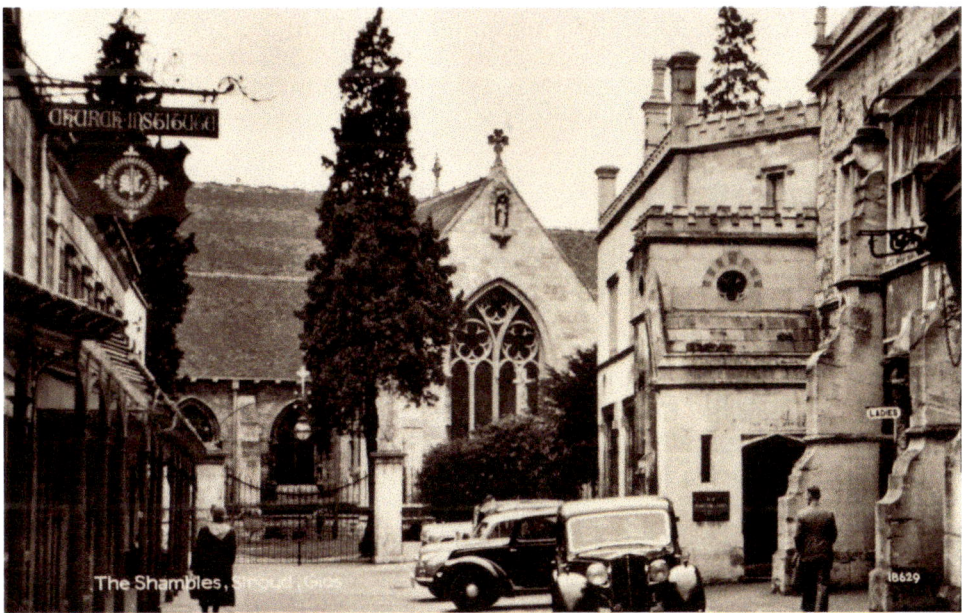

The Shambles, Stroud, where the market is held.

ceased, there is still a vestige of the industry in a small outlet producing cloth for billiard tables and tennis balls even today. Stroud mostly deals in light engineering and small-scale manufacturing in the twenty-first century. There is even a factory producing fake snow for films and television dramas called Snow Business!

Sudeley

Sudeley Castle (very near Winchcombe) is an impressive and romantic building which is Grade I listed, in part ruined, but the rest dating mainly from the fifteenth century. Ironically its name derives from the Old English 'scydd' meaning shed – the whole word meaning 'a clearing with a shed'! King Ethelred had a Saxon manor house on this site and by the twelfth century a castle had been built here – and in fact in the thirteenth century William de Sudeley was one of the four knights responsible for executing Thomas Becket in Canterbury Cathedral.

The earliest parts of the building date from 1442. Ralph Boteler, an English baron, built a castle with accommodation for servants, men at arms and family on the site of a previous one. Edward IV, when he came to the throne, took guardianship of the castle, unjustly accusing Boteler of treason. It is said as he was led away Boteler cried 'Sudeley Castle, thou art the traitor not I.' It was then given to Edward's brother who was to be Richard III and he used it as a base for the Battle of Tewkesbury.

The castle was once again important during Henry VIII's reign, so much so that he brought both Catherine of Aragon and Anne Boleyn here. When he visited with Anne in 1535 the castle had been empty for a while. He also met Thomas Cromwell at nearby Winchcombe on a different occasion to discuss the Dissolution of the Monasteries. Katherine Parr, Henry's sixth wife, is associated with Sudeley as she moved here when she secretly married Thomas Seymour (who owned the castle from 1547) after Henry died. Catherine died in childbirth and is buried under a marble tomb in St Mary's Chapel at Sudeley. Rare copies of her books are on display in one of the rooms.

Elizabeth I came on three visits and in 1592 celebrated the anniversary of the defeat of the Armada. Charles I took refuge here during outbreaks of hostilities between the Royalists and Parliamentarians. King George III visited in 1788 when he fell down a broken flight of stairs but fortunately landed on a housekeeper!

Sudeley was neglected after the Civil War and became derelict until it was rescued in 1837 by Worcester industrialists John and William Dent. They began the restoration and this was continued by their descendants, notably their niece Emma Dent who enhanced the castle with period antiques. The castle is now owned by Elizabeth, Lady Ashcombe and her family who have worked on restoring the gardens. It is a glamorous venue for weddings these days and Elizabeth Hurley married Arun Nayar, an Indian textile heir, in a private chapel here – their guests dressed in pink.

S

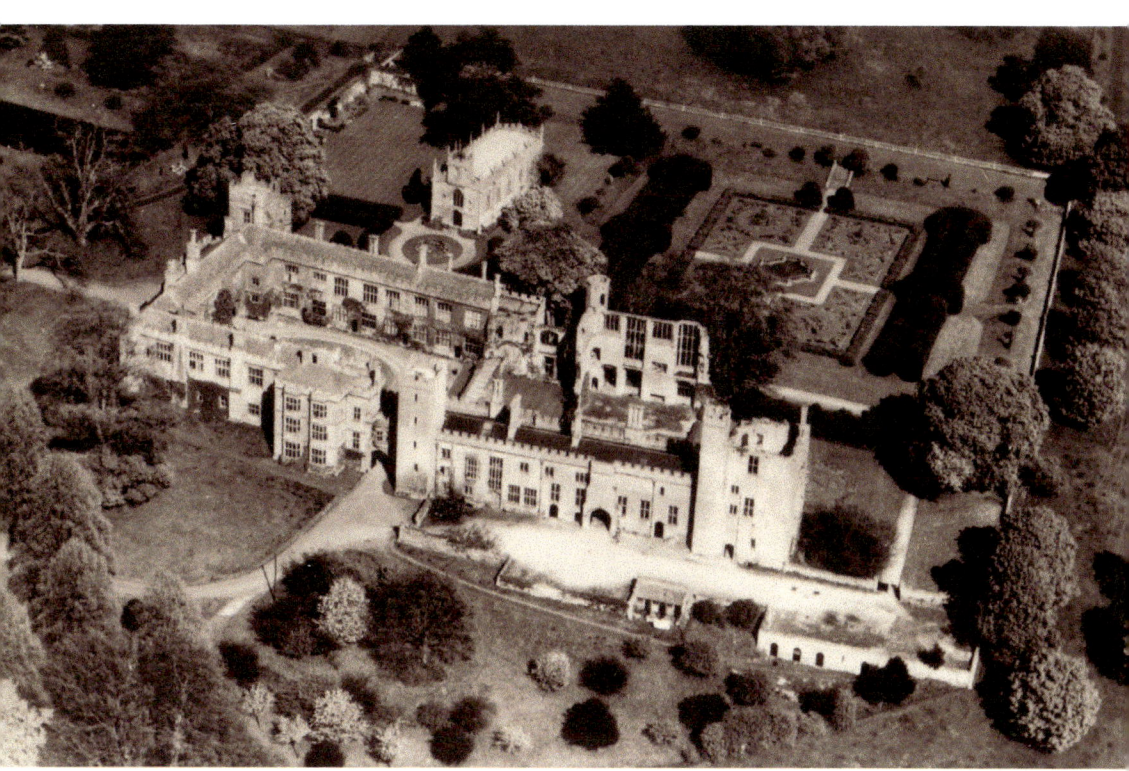

Sudeley Castle.

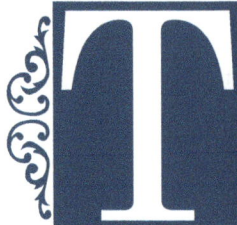

Tetbury

Ten miles south-west of Cirencester is the town of Tetbury, the local town to Prince Charles's home of Highgrove. In fact there is a Highgrove shop on the main street selling all sorts of lovely things, from tea towels and oven gloves to books, high-class groceries and gardening accessories.

In the middle of the town, which makes it so recognisable, is the seventeenth-century market building or 'town hall' with its three rows of Tuscan pillars and stone roof all topped off with gilded dolphins (dolphins are part of the town crest). The high street is not very extensive but there are some interesting independent shops and it is renowned for its antique and bric-a-brac shops. There is also the Police Bygones

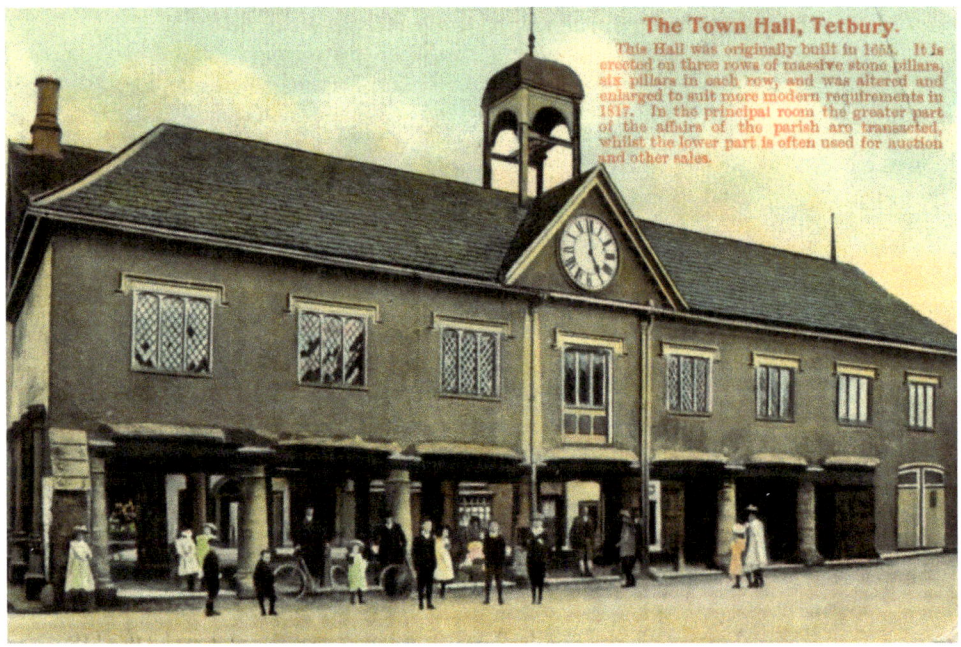

The seventeenth-century Market House.

Museum hidden amongst the retailers. Near the market building is the Snooty Fox Hotel, rebuilt in the nineteenth century by the Westonbirt architect Lewis Vulliamy. Apparently there was a ballroom on the first floor to entertain the Beaufort Hunt originally, but this has long since been divided up into bedrooms. Behind the Snooty Fox away from the main street is the old market place, the 'Chipping', which was once a wool-collecting centre for cloth towns to the north and west. Maybe this is why the wool-sack races are held here every spring, although this is unlikely as the event only dates back to the 1970s. A 60-lb sack of wool is carried up and down Gumstool Hill (at speed) on Bank Holiday Monday, the last Monday in May. Mostly the square is overlooked quietly by the seventeenth- and eighteenth-century buildings around it.

The Gothic eighteenth-century church of St Mary the Virgin and St Mary Magdalene on the outskirts of Tetbury still has its original medieval tower and spire, which can be seen from miles around. The inside of the church, though rather spooky, is lit by the Perpendicular windows, shedding light on the panelled gallery and box pews within.

Tewkesbury

On the periphery of our area is Tewkesbury (originally Theocsbury after Theoc who founded a hermitage here in the seventh century), 10 miles from Gloucester, and is worth visiting because of its glorious abbey which sets it apart from other towns. The great Benedictine abbey was founded by the Norman Robert Fitzharnon who imported stone from Caen to build it; however he died fourteen years before its consecration in 1107. His son-in-law Robert Fitzroy, Earl of Gloucester, continued to take an interest in the project. Because of the endowments and support of the de Clare family the abbey became one of the most powerful religious houses in the land, owning land in the Cotswolds as well as large tithe barns in the area.

The abbey was the focal point of the town and was responsible for its prosperity during the Middle Ages. However at the Dissolution of the Monasteries it was sold to the parishioners for a meagre £453. The town is bordered by the rivers Severn and Avon and on the east and south sides by abbey lands, but still managed to grow in density in the seventeenth and eighteenth centuries. The abbey still overshadows the town with its 46-foot-square Norman tower, which is 132 feet high. The 65-foot-high recessed arch of the west front is one of the largest ever constructed. There was a wooden spire on the tower which took its height to 260 feet, but it blew down in 1559.

To the south of the abbey, off Lincoln Green Lane, is the 'Bloody Meadow' where one of the 'bloodiest and most decisive battles of the Wars of the Roses' was fought. The Lancastrian army of Margaret of Anjou were slaughtered by the Yorkists on 4 May 1417. Her son Edward was slain and Margaret herself was imprisoned in the Tower of London until ransomed by her father, the King of France. The battle is mentioned in Shakespeare's *Richard III*.

A-Z of the Cotswolds

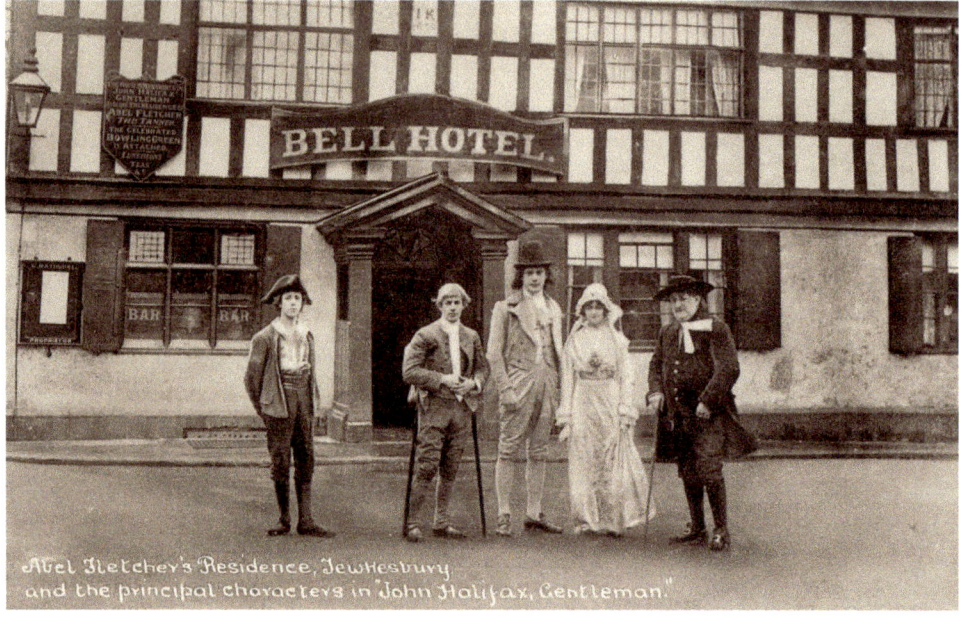

The Bell Hotel, Tewkesbury.

There are interesting medieval and Tudor buildings in the town. The Black Bear public house dates from 1308 but unfortunately is now closed and, such are the times, is unlikely to reopen. The Baptist Chapel is a timber-framed building dating back to the fifteenth century but didn't become a chapel as such until the seventeenth century. The Abbey Mill is written about in Mrs Craik's novel *John Halifax, Gentleman* where it becomes Abel Fletcher's Mill in Norton Bury (Tewkesbury). More recent buildings of interest are John Moore's museum about the novelist and natural history of the area, the Roses Theatre where Eric Morecombe gave his final appearance, and the various shops selling Tewkesbury mustard. Tewkesbury mustard brought prosperity to the town in the seventeenth century and is a blend of mustard and horse radish.

Tyndale Monument

This 111-foot tower was built on Nibley Knoll in 1866 to commemorate William Tyndale who translated the New Testament into English in the sixteenth century. By doing this he made the text accessible to the common man, but this was very controversial as it was thought that the teachings of the text should only happen through the intermediary of a priest. As a result he was burnt as a heretic, but only two years after his death there was an English Bible in every parish church in England.

North Nibley would like to lay claim to Tyndale but it is more likely that he was born at Slimbridge. There is a plaque on the tower which reads 'Erected AD 1866 in grateful remembrance of William Tyndale who first caused the New Testament to be printed in the Mother Tongue of his countrymen. Born near this spot he suffered martyrdom in Vilvorde in Flanders Oct 6 1536'. It is possible to climb to the top of the tower by a spiral staircase of 121 steps. The views from the top are spectacular, especially towards the River Severn; likewise the tower stands out for miles on its hilltop perch and is visible from Thornbury and, it is said, even Bristol. The Cotswold Way passes at the foot of the tower, descending the hill and into North Nibley itself.

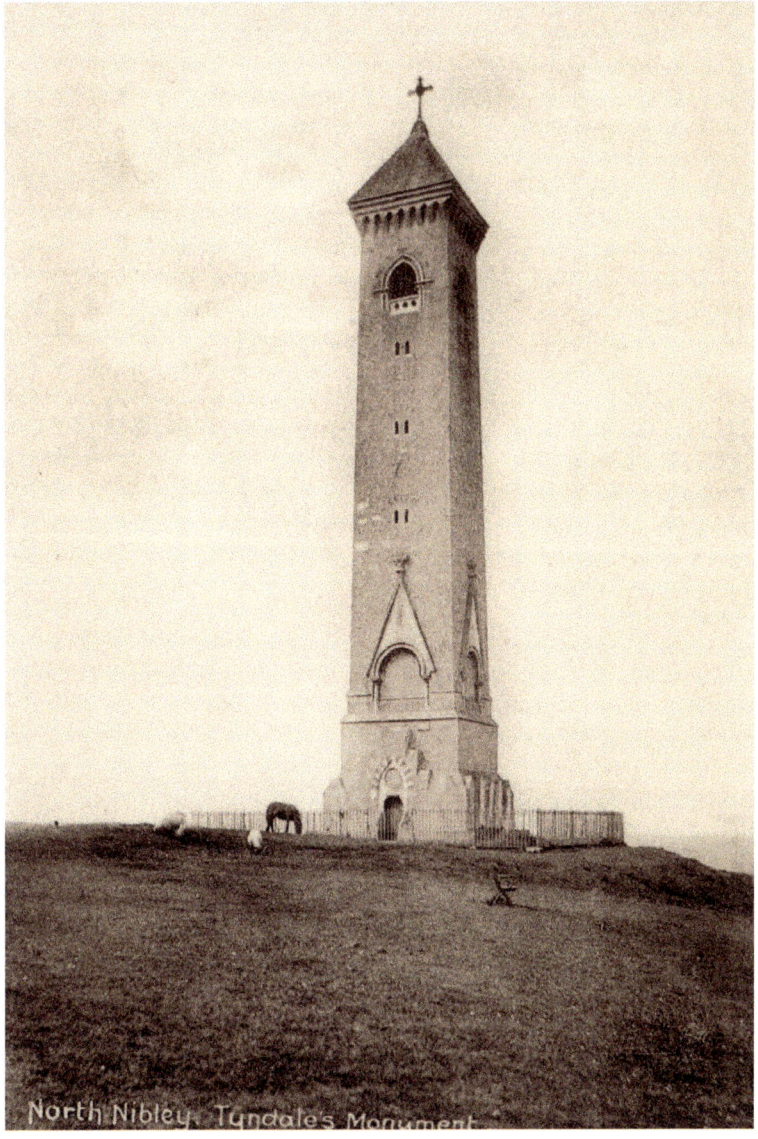

The Tyndale Monument, North Nibley.

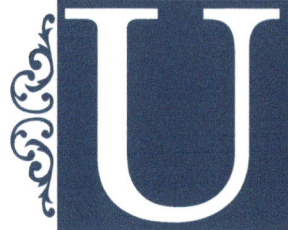

Uley

Uley (Euulege in the Domesday Book) is situated in a low wooded valley outside of Dursley on the Stroud road, and is surrounded by beautiful hilly countryside. It was a successful cloth town before the Industrial Revolution, producing the famous 'Uley blue' cloth for military uniforms and smart clothing – there are some lovely eighteenth-century houses reflecting this prosperity. It has a fine nineteenth-century church, St Giles's (on the site of previous Norman and Saxon buildings), designed by the architect S. S. Teulon, who was responsible for the Tyndale Monument.

Uley has its own brewery which produces 'Old Spot Ale', which can be enjoyed at the eighteenth-century Old Crown pub near the green. This is the only hostelry remaining from a total of fourteen once found in the village! Uley has its own arts centre, Prema, founded in 1970 in the old Baptist Chapel, running art and craft classes as well as offering theatre and music events.

In 1918 a lady called Alyce Cunningham adopted a gorilla called John Daniel, or Jonathan, which her brother had bought for £300 in London. It could often be seen sitting in her car as she drove around Uley during the four years he lived with her, before growing into an adult, at which point he was sold to an American. It is proposed a sculpture will be erected to the popular Jonathan somewhere in the village.

Just outside Uley is Stouts Hill, the neo-Gothic home of antiquary Samuel Rudder, which was run as a preparatory school in the late twentieth century attended by Mark Phillips, Stephen Fry and Rik Mayall. Nearby is Downham Hill, also known as 'Smallpox Hill' because of the isolation hospital that was sited there. If you follow the footpath near the church up the hillside you will find yourself at the Iron Age settlement of Uley Bury with fantastic views of the surrounding countryside. Further along the hillside in a grassy field is Hetty Pegler's Tump – 6,000 years old and pre-dating the fortifications of Uley Bury by thirty-four centuries, having been built in 3700 BC. The Tump was probably a chieftain's family's burial site and it is possible to go through the entrance hole and get some impression of the stone-built chamber inside.

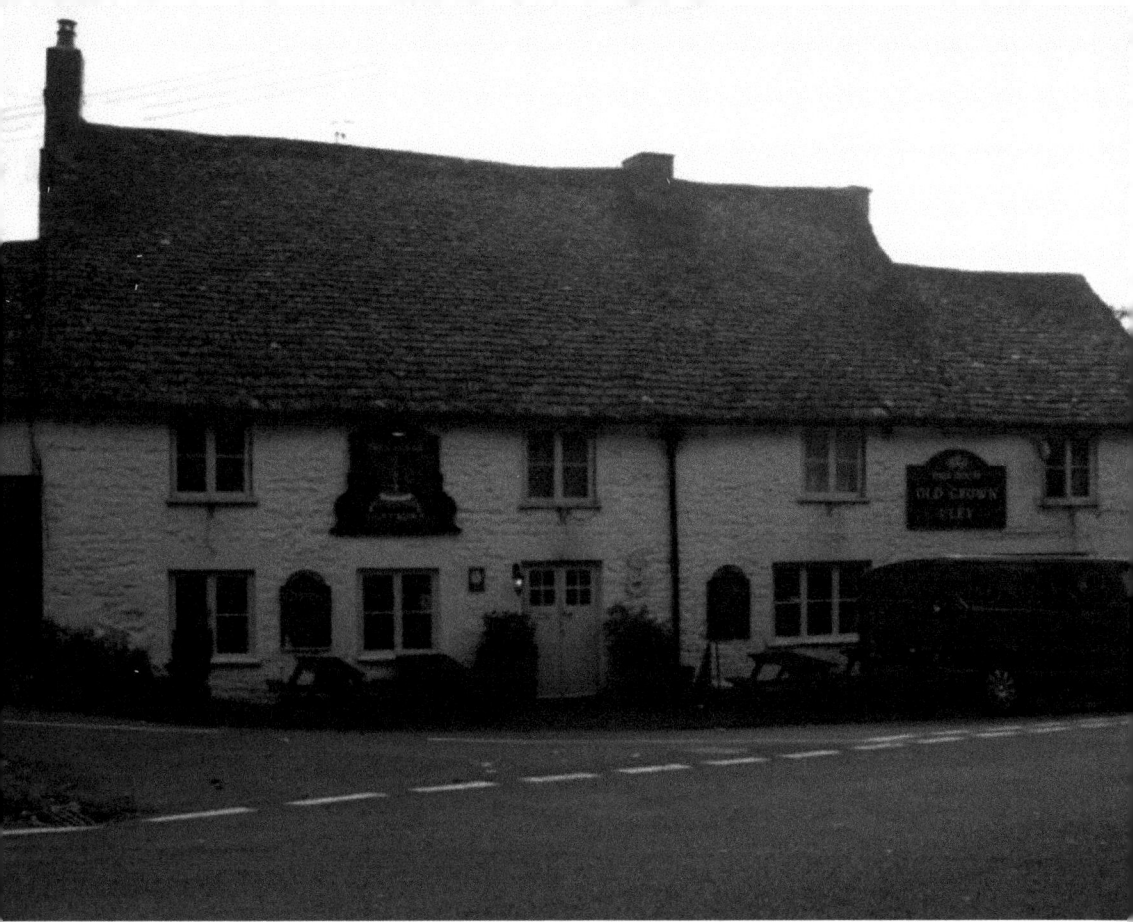

The Old Crown at Uley.

Vales

Adjacent and to the west of the Cotswold area are the vales of Berkeley, Gloucester and Evesham. Berkeley and Gloucester vales are on the River Severn whilst Evesham is on the River Avon. The vales were important growing regions because the rivers kept the temperatures equable. The vales of Berkeley and Gloucester were dairying regions while Evesham was (and is) famous for the 'blossom trail' as there was an abundance of fruit trees. Berkeley Vale was famous for its 'Double Gloucester' cheese, although this was first made in Gloucester itself in 1498 and originally from sheep's milk. The handsome rich brown cows with noticeable white stripe known as Gloucester cattle, now rare, produced special milk with small globules of fat. Single Gloucester cheese was made from the morning's full-cream milk and skimmed milk in the evening and was kept for domestic consumption, while the superior Double Gloucester was made from the morning and evening's full-cream milk and coloured with annatto. This would have been taken to market. Another local breed was the Old Spot pig, which was an orchard pig bred in the Berkeley area. It was said that its meat tasted of apples! It was kept in the Cotswolds.

There has been a revival in artisan cheesemaking and therefore a revival of cheeses like the Double Gloucester, and hopefully this will promote the keeping of the rare breed Gloucester cattle. To see these gorgeous animals close up visit Adam Henson's Cotswold Farm Park. Incidentally, truckles of Double Gloucester cheese were hurled down Coopers Hill for the contestants to scramble after in Gloucester's famous cheese-rolling event.

Villas

Curiosity was aroused when a farmer, trying to dig his ferret out of a rabbit hole in 1864, came across bits of mosaic and pottery shards. The landowner decided to excavate further and Chedworth Roman Villa was discovered. It was in a beautiful wooded part of the Coln Valley and is one of the finest examples of a Roman villa

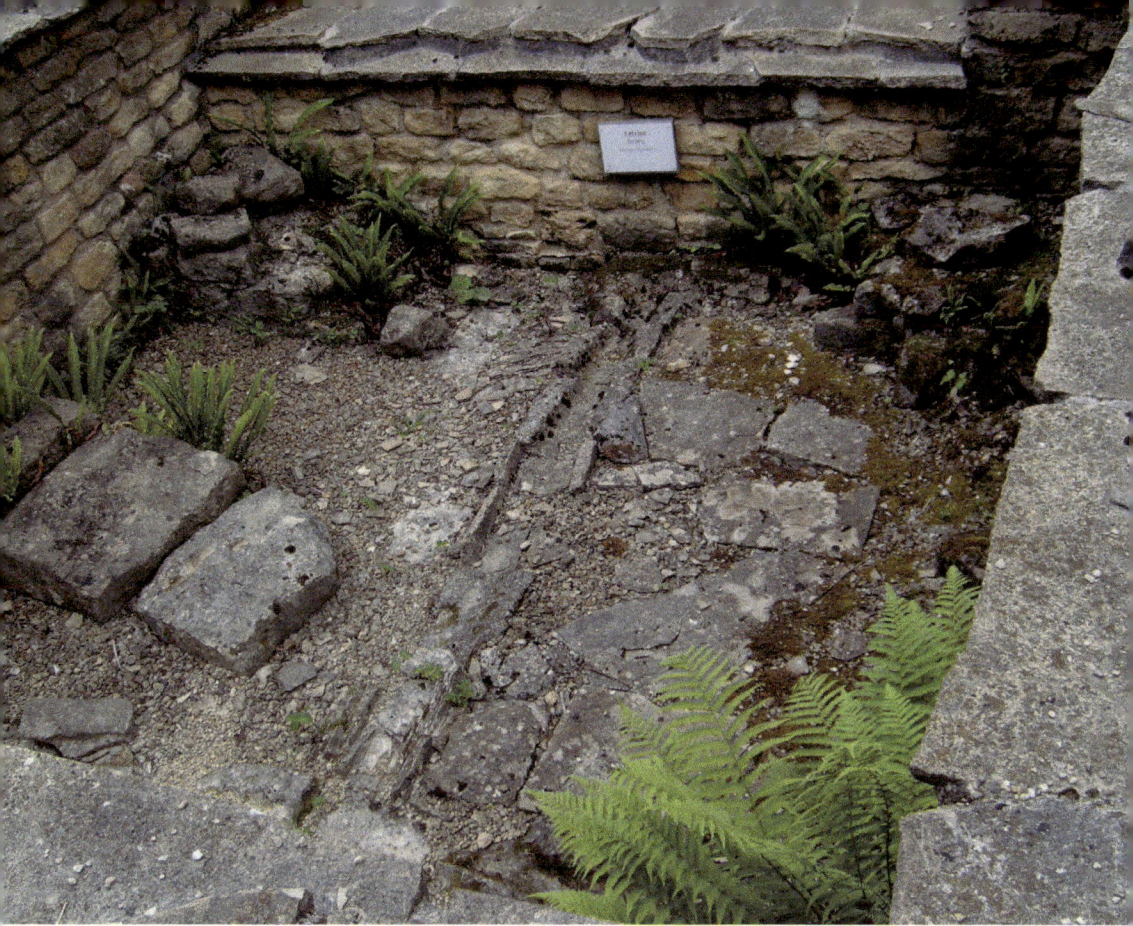

The latrine, Chedworth Roman Villa.

in Britain, dating from around AD 130. Since 1924 it has been in the hands of the National Trust and boasts a hypocaust system, bath suites and mosaic pavements. In the west wing the mosaic is of the four seasons. There is a museum telling the story of Roman Britain and a shop.

In the churchyard at Woodchester, 2 miles south of Stroud, is Woodchester's greatest claim to fame: the remains of a 'luxurious Roman Villa' including a mosaic of the *Myth of Orpheus*. Here Orpheus plays a lyre in the centre of two rings of animals. It was excavated by Samuel Lyons, Gloucestershire's antiquary in 1766, and used to be uncovered every ten years until it was decided to make a replica. Brothers Bob and John Woodward made a copy with more than 1.5 million pieces of stone, having been inspired by the original. This was displayed in Wotton-under-Edge, then Prinknash Abbey, before being auctioned in 2010 for £75,000.

At Witcombe, near Brockworth and Painswick, is a first-century Roman villa around three sides of a courtyard on a terrace below woodlands with extensive views towards the Severn. There is a small mosaic pavement here of dolphins and seahorses. To see more Roman finds go to Cirencester's Corinium Museum.

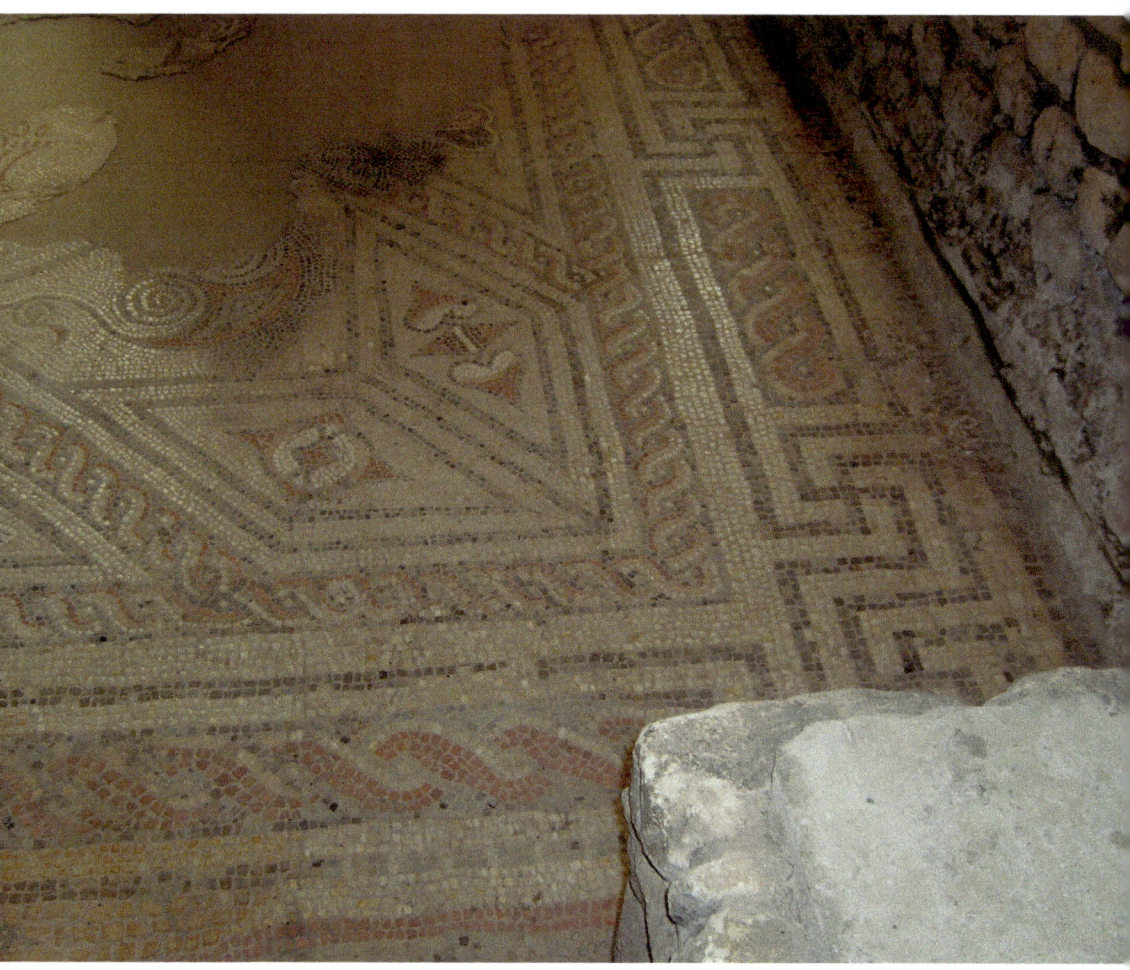
Roman mosaic at Chedworth Roman Villa.

Whittington

Whittington is 4 miles east of Cheltenham and is a small village to the south of Cleeve Hill. There is a row of cottages with a Victorian well labelled 'waste not, want not'. Beneath the high walls of the sixteenth-century Whittington Court, once the manor house, is the church of St Bartholomew's, away from the village itself. Dating back to Norman times, the church has a small bell-cote and an attractive north porch but most fascinating of all are the three fourteenth-century effigies of two knights and a lady. There is a 1556 brass to Richard Cotton and his wife, builders of Whittington Court. The head-stops to the arcading are two little Chaucerian-looking figures of a gentleman and lady.

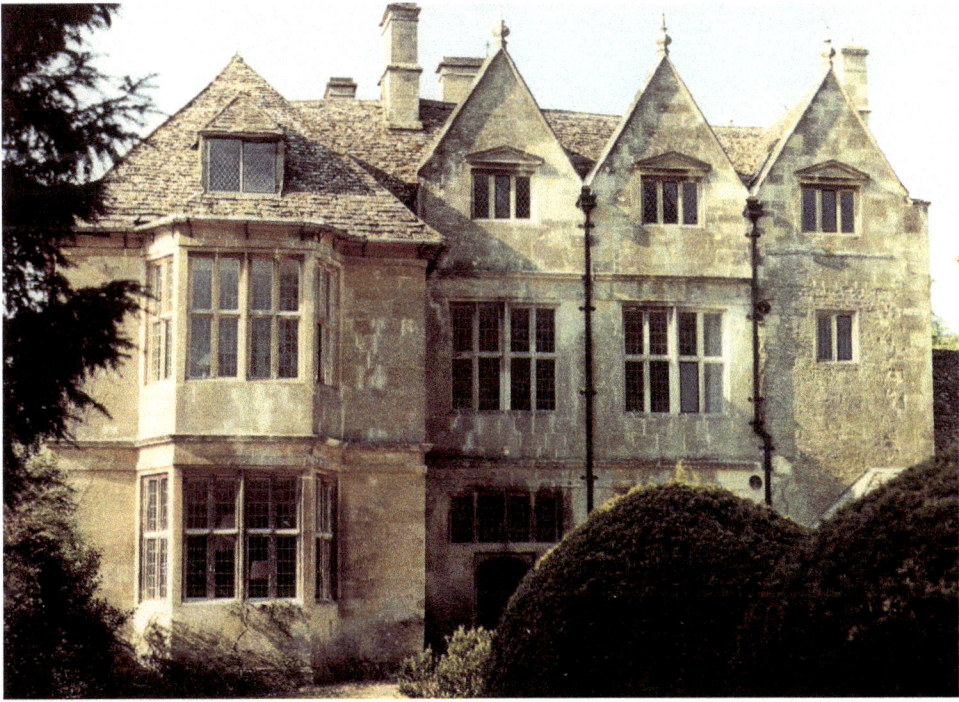

Whittington Court.

A-Z of the Cotswolds

Winchcombe

Sheltered on three sides by somewhat wooded hills, Winchcombe is 6 miles north-east of Cheltenham but is in the local authority district of Tewkesbury. The area has some history as Belas Knap Neolithic long barrow is situated above the town, constructed in 3000 BC. An abbey was founded here in 798 by King Kenulf of Mercia and many pilgrims came to the shrine of his son, Saint Kenelm.

Winchcombe was capital of its own shire until it became part of Gloucestershire in the eleventh century. In the twelfth century a motte-and-bailey castle was built here by Roger Fitzmiles, 2nd Earl of Hereford, for Empress Mathilda, but the site is unknown. In the thirteenth century a great Benedictine abbey was established which grew in power because of the number or pilgrims visiting, its proximity to Sudeley Castle and its extensive sheep pastures.

There is a fine Perpendicular wool church, St Peter's, which although built by parishioners in the 1450s, had a nave provided by Sir Ralph Boteler of Sudeley Castle and a chancel by the abbot. Despite its connections to the abbey, which was close by, it outlived the Dissolution. It has a fine west tower which is surmounted by a gilded

The high street, Winchcombe.

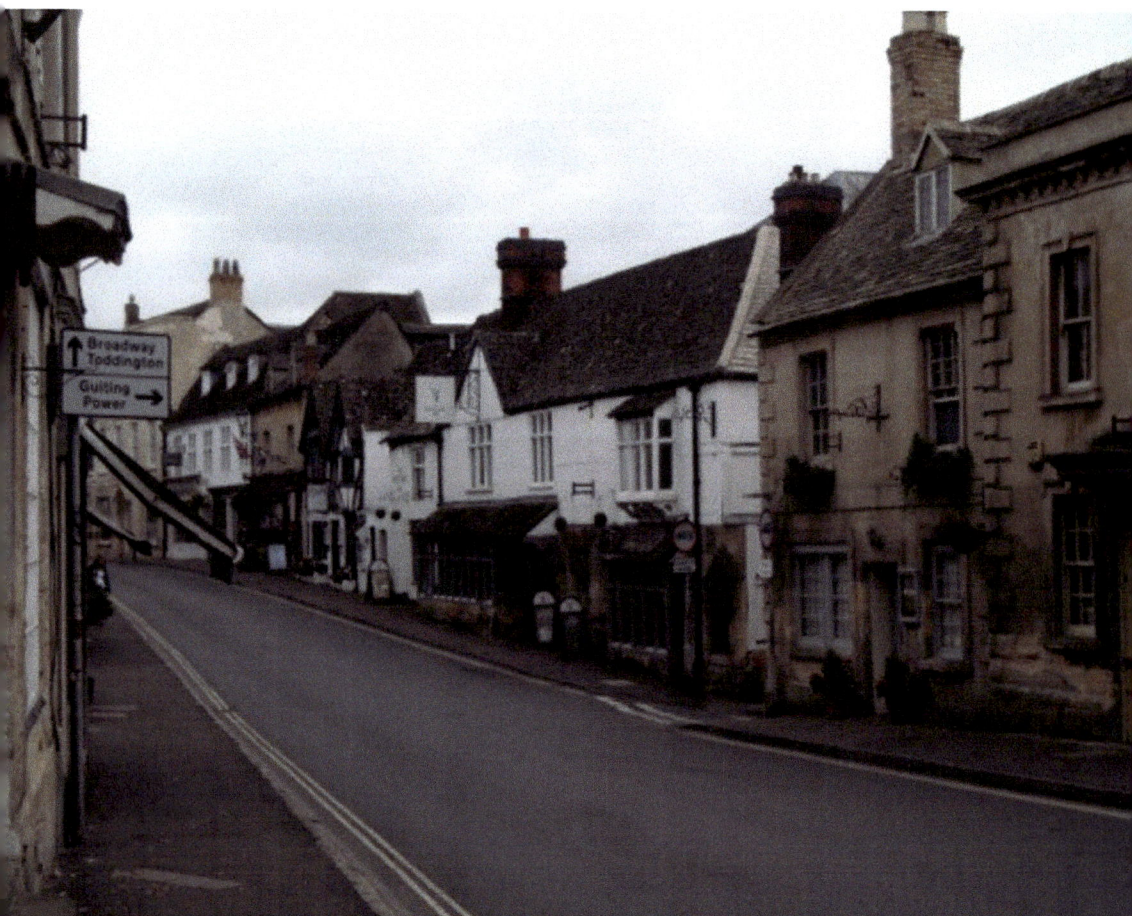

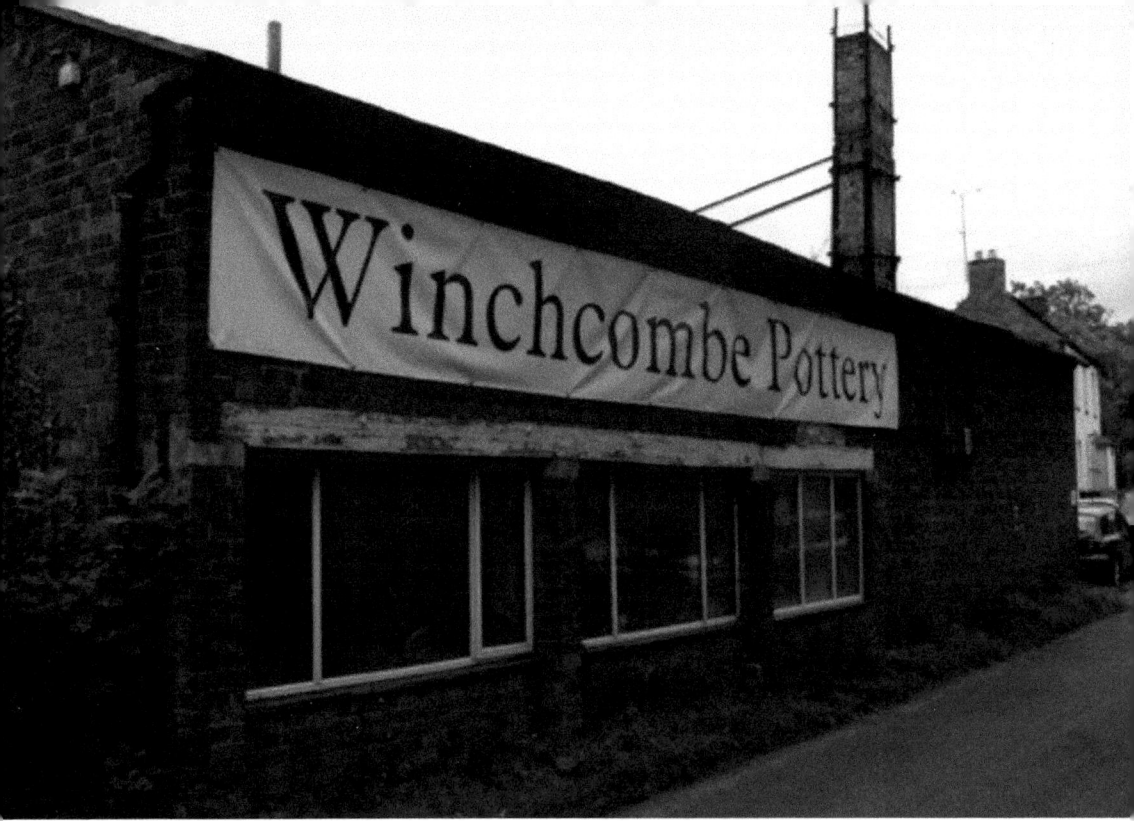

Michael Cardew revived the Greet pottery in 1926 and it became Winchcombe Pottery.

weathercock that once belonged to St Mary Redcliffe Church in Bristol. There are some fifteenth-century screens gracing the inside of the church, some floor tiles from the abbey, a seventeenth-century holy table, and George III's coat of arms on the wall. There is a poignant monument to the knight Sir Thomas Williams who left a space for his widow by the prayer desk where he is kneeling, but it remains empty as she remarried.

Lord Seymour of Sudeley was responsible for destroying Winchcombe Abbey at the Dissolution but a reminder of its existence is the medieval George Inn on the high street, which was the hostel for pilgrims, and on the doorway is carved the coat of arms of the 16th abbot, Richard of Kidderminster.

The Restoration was a time of poverty for Winchcombe and during this time it was known for cattle rustling and all sorts of lawlessness. Tobacco was grown in an attempt to make money, but this had been outlawed since the Commonwealth, so troops were sent on horseback to trample the crop. Appropriately there is a museum of police memorabilia in the town and the old stocks can still be found in a small fenced enclosure.

Witney

On both sides of the Windrush, 7 miles east of Burford and 13 miles west of Oxford, is the old woollen town of Witney. The town made blankets from the time of Edward III until 2002 when the fashion for duvets undermined the trade.

Witney is the largest market town in Oxfordshire and its name derives from the Old English for 'Witta's island'. It was known as Wyttannige in a Saxon charter of 469 and Witenie in the Domesday Book of 1086. In his *Natural History of 1677* Dr Plot states, 'No place yields blanketing so notoriously white as is made at Witney.' The water for blanket making came from the River Windrush. Even Native Americans had a preference for Witney blankets, which they bought at the remote Hudson Bay Trading Company. A charter was granted to the Company of Blanket Weavers in 1721 – so the mills were founded four centuries ago. The Blanket Hall on the high street was built in the eighteenth century for the weighing and measuring of blankets. At the height of production there were five blanket factories.

The buildings in the town reflect the time of prosperity. There is a seventeenth-century Butter Cross and an eighteenth-century Town Hall. Church Green has some attractive seventeenth- and eighteenth-century houses while at the far end is the huge tower and 150-foot spire of the thirteenth-century church. In Wood Green a nineteenth-century mill has been converted into apartments. The reputation of Witney blankets carried the trade through the Industrial Revolution. Even the local football team was known as the 'blanket-men'. The town also made mops and at one time every ship in the Royal Navy had a Witney mop. But although the blanket trade

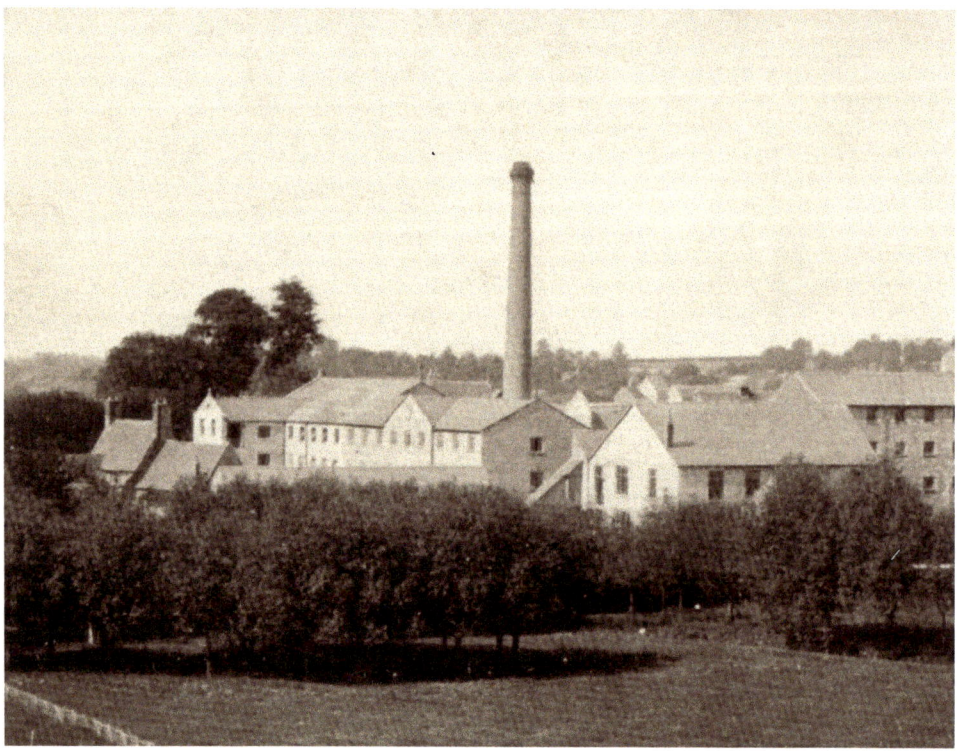

The old blanket factories, Witney.

survived into the twentieth century, it just limped into the twenty-first when the last factory, Early's, closed in 2002. It was demolished and now new housing estates cover the site.

The museum in Court Mews tells Witney's story and that of the surrounding countryside. South-east of Witney is the Cogges Farm Museum, which is an Edwardian farm exhibiting equipment and livestock. In Cogges church are the monuments to the Blake family who owned the farm, while above them is a frieze of monsters – even some with human heads!

X – Crossroads: Tom Long's Signpost

Tom Long's Post is a signpost at the convergence of a number of minor roads crossing Minchinhampton Common. It is said that Tom Long was an eighteenth-century highwayman who was hung there for his crimes. However, as the local gallows were at Over or Gloucester Gaol, it is more likely that his dead body was displayed in chains there as a deterrent. Another story told by Colonel Yarnold of Minchinhampton is that Tom Long was the nickname for a carrier and that the site was a dropping-off place on the Stroud to London road. However, in a lecture given in 1874, Charles Payne said that at the beginning of the nineteenth century Tom Long committed suicide by

Tom Long's Post – the crossroads on Minchinhampton Common.

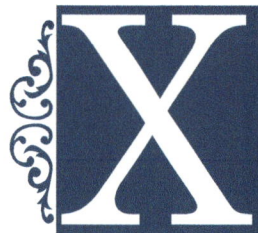

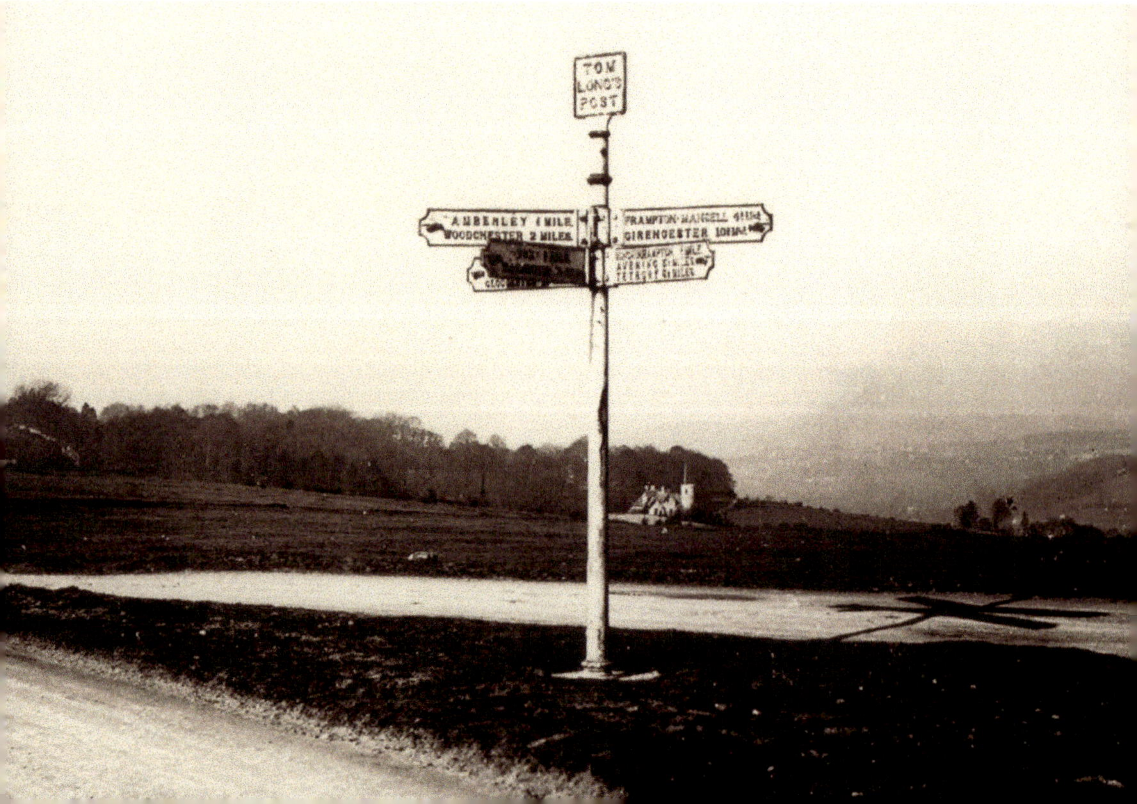

hanging himself in a cottage near a Rodborough Manor. This is an interesting theory for there is a long-held belief that suicides should be buried at crossroads. This is because suicide was once a crime – incredibly up until 1962. It was thought that a suicide was an unquiet soul and that the ghosts of people who died by suicide were hostile and susceptible to demonic control. Clergyman Montague Summer said in 1926: 'When a ghost from a body issues forth from the grave and finds there are four paths stretching in as many directions he will be puzzled to know which way to take ... until dawn compels him to return to the earth, woe betide the unhappy being who happens to pass by when he is lingering there perplexed and confused.' It was also thought that a stake through the heart would 'pin' the restless soul to the spot.

Y

Yanworth

Yanworth lies 2 miles west of Northleach, 14 miles south-east of Cheltenham and overlooks the bosky valley of the River Coln. The small church of St Michael's, dating from 1200, can be found amongst farm buildings. It has a Norman doorway with chevron carvings, an original chancel and a tub font. There is a wall painting of Old Father Time with his scythe. A nineteenth-century Grade II listed barn is 15 yards away from the farmhouse. Yanworth is on the Macmillan Way and is part of the Stowell Park estate owned by Lord Vestey. Chedworth Roman Villa is nearby.

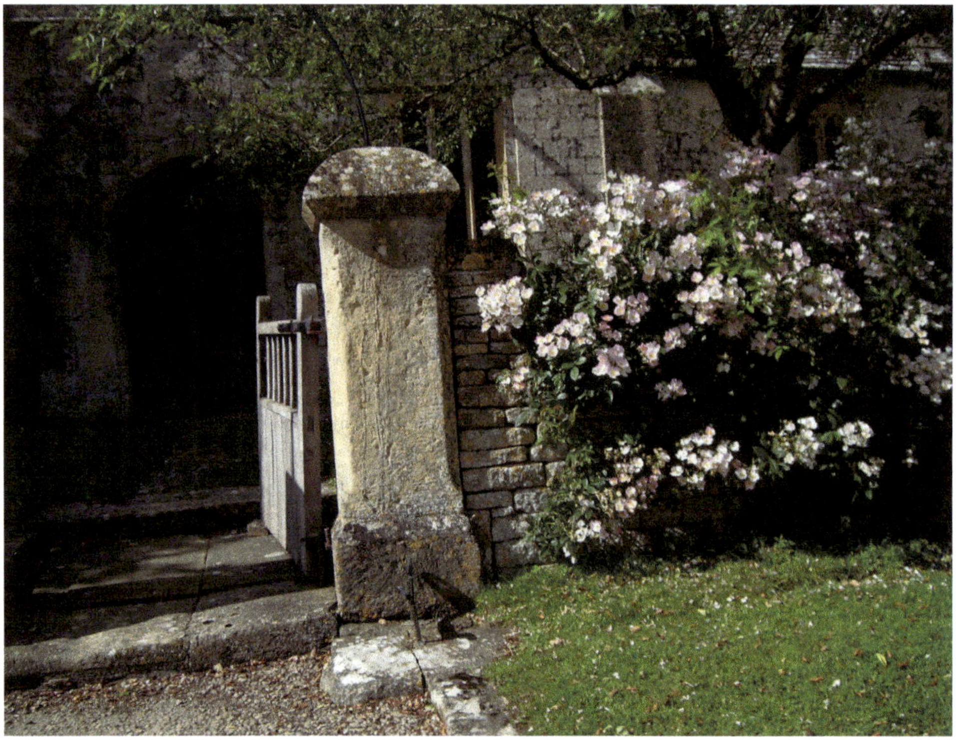

St Michael's Church, Yanworth, can be found in a farmyard!

Z

Zebras in the Cotswolds

It's true, there are zebras in the Cotswolds – at the Cotswold Wildlife Park, 3 miles south of Burford. This rather superior zoo, dealing with one of the largest collections of animals in Great Britain, was started in 1970. There are 200 acres of gardens and parkland around Bradwell Grove, as well as an early nineteenth-century Tudor-style mansion. There is plenty of room for the rhinos to roam the lawn, and there are enclosures for ostriches, zebras and giraffes. The smaller mammals like the meerkats are in a walled garden area. Cotswold Wildlife Park runs an endangered species breeding programme whereby it exchanges animals with other zoos and it takes part in critical conservation projects around the world. It is a privately owned zoo which relies on its visitors to pay its way and it has a vibrant education program. In addition it has a narrow-gauge railway, picnic areas, an adventure playground and a licensed restaurant for a fulfilling day out. There are fascinating owls in the wooded area – but watch out for those zebras in the Cotswolds!

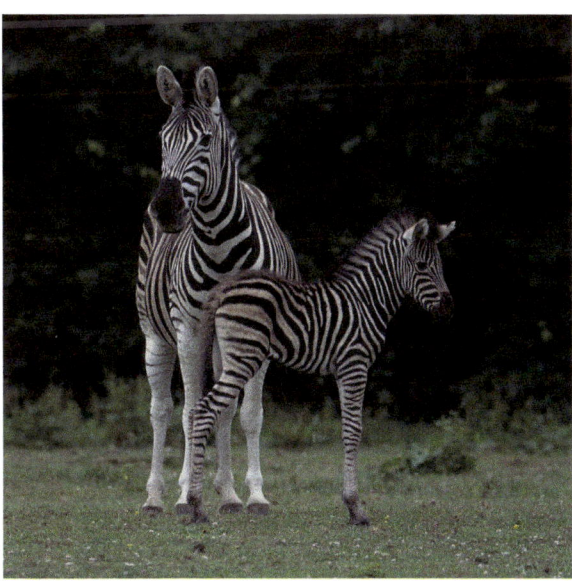

Zebras at the Cotswold Wildlife Park near Burford.

Acknowledgements

Many thanks are due to the following for donating photographs (and copyright remains with the donors):
Franca Giampa, Randwick
Harry Tubbs, Kingscote
Richard Martin, Cotswold Woollen Weavers
Edward Peake, Sezincote
Hugo Mander, Owlpen Manor
Mary Clark, Kelmscott
Debbie, Cotswold Farm Park
Tanya, The College Arms, Lower Quinton
Other photos are by Sue Hazeldine and Kim Hazeldine